Writing and Publishing
Books for Children
in the 1990s

WRITING AND PUBLISHING BOOKS FOR CHILDREN IN THE 1990s

The Inside Story
from the Editor's Desk

Olga Litowinsky

WALKER AND COMPANY   NEW YORK

First published in the United States of America in 1992
by Walker Publishing Company, Inc.

Published simultaneously in Canada by Thomas Allen & Son
Canada, Limited, Markham, Ontario

LIBRARY OF CONGRESS CATALOGING-IN-PUBLICATION DATA
Litowinsky, Olga.
Writing and publishing books for children in the 1990s : the
inside story from the editor's desk / Olga Litowinsky.
p.   cm.
Includes index.
ISBN 0-8027-8130-6.   ISBN 0-8027-7375-3 (pbk.)
1. Children's literature—Authorship. 2. Children's literature.
—Marketing. I. Title.
PN147.5.L58   1992
808.06′8—dc20   91-29772
CIP

Text design by Michael Chesworth
Illustrations by Elivia Savadier

Printed in the United States of America

2   4   6   8   10   9   7   5   3

In memory of
Jacqueline Sweetman Litowinsky
1931–1991

Respect the child, respect him to the end, but also respect yourself. Be the companion of his thought, the friend of his friendship, the lover of his virtue—but no kinsman of his sin.

—RALPH WALDO EMERSON

CONTENTS

Part I. Before Acceptance

Part II. And After

ACKNOWLEDGMENTS

This book is the result of over thirty years' editing experience, a long apprenticeship under many gifted editors and writers. Since I cannot begin to thank them all for their help in the past, let me at least thank those who have helped me in the writing and research of this book, from my sister-in-law, Jacqueline Litowinsky, who read the first draft, to my editor, Bebe Willoughby, who remained tactful and encouraging all the way, and Patricia Reilly Giff, Grace Clarke, Dagmar Greve, Anne Mao, Marilyn Marlow, George Nicholson, Pat Orvis, Michelle Poploff, Jim Roginski, John Sargent, Janis Skreen, Ron Buehl, and Helene Steinhauer, who gave me their invaluable suggestions for improvement.

Most of all I want to thank the writers with whom I've worked over the years: they were my best teachers.

PREFACE

We are in an exciting time, a good time to begin a writing career. But if you wish to write—and publish—a children's book in the 1990s, it's important to understand the changes that have taken place, especially during the last fifteen years, in this stimulating and fulfilling field. Although most of the old rules still obtain, today there are more opportunities than ever for writers of different kinds of books for children because of the growth of the paperback side of publishing, juvenile book clubs, expanding shelf space in general bookstores, and a growing number of children's-only bookstores. Many neophyte writers still think a children's book is a picture book, when in reality the field is extremely diverse. By understanding this diversity you will increase your chances of selling your work.

Since many of you already know the basics, I've decided to address myself in greater depth to other questions you, the writer, may have. I'm assuming you already know, for example, that manuscripts should be typed double spaced on white bond. But do you know the best way to submit a manuscript written and printed with a word processor? And what can make *your* manuscript stand out from the rest on an editor's desk? In the chapter entitled "Secrets from the Slush Pile," you'll see information about how to submit a manuscript, but you'll also find out about multiple submissions and the reason why correct spelling and grammar can make a difference.

For those who care about page or word counts, I've provided that information. But I also discuss the kinds of books editors are looking for—and why. I hope to help the published writer, who needs to know more about the editorial process and the publishing industry.

Writing for children is a noble calling, but today, more than ever, it is a profitable business. None of us can afford to forget, however, that it is a business that depends on writers, for without books to sell publishers would cease to exist. You are important to

editors because without books not only would we be out of wonderful jobs, our lives would be poorer intellectually and spiritually.

Some of our best friends are books, and we all hope to meet
yours one day on our desks, at the library, or in the bookstore.
Writers and editors are in this endeavor together, and let us pray
that we may go on doing our best in the field we love forever.

PART I
Before Acceptance

1 Secrets of the Slush Pile

YOU ARE WRITING a book—or have finished one—and don't have an agent. Now you want to get it published. You may have decided to send it to the address on the copyright page of one of your favorite books or you may have found the name and address of a publisher somewhere else. So you mail it off to a publisher. Now begins a period of anticipation and dread.

We all have the same fantasy. The envelope arrives in an editorial office. An editor sees it and opens it. She begins to read while standing at the office mailbox. She walks with it, still reading, back to her desk and spends the rest of the day sipping cold coffee and turning the pages. "Eureka!" she cries at last. "This is brilliant. I want to buy it." And she telephones you immediately and promises to send you a contract and check within a few days.

The reality is that you wait because your manuscript is in the slush pile. You check the mail every day. Weeks go by, then months, and sometimes even years. Surely she's had time to read it by *now*, you think. Life goes on, and maybe one day you receive the manuscript with a polite form letter saying. "Thanks, but no thanks." That's when you despair, file away the manuscript, and feel too embarrassed to send it out again. Has this happened to you? Take heart: this chapter will change all that. But first a story.

Years ago, when I was an assistant editor, I wrote my first book: it was about a pigeon that wanted to be a seagull. The story was inspired by a newspaper story about a pigeon found on the beach, its leg caught in a clam. In my story, the pigeon sailed down the Hudson River on a passing yacht to the sea, found a beach, got caught by a clam, and then was rescued by a young man named

Tom, who took the pigeon sailing with him on his boat. Rosemary Wells, who was working at Macmillan as a designer, enthusiastically illustrated my dummy. Well, just like everybody else who's ever written a children's book, I knew the book was brilliant—and the superb sketches by Rosemary didn't hurt it, either. Ah, youth, ignorance, and naïveté! All three came along with me when I showed our dummy to an editor who was kind enough to look at the work of her colleagues.

"It's derivative," she said. "There are thousands of books about something wanting to be something else." I nodded. I'd read hundreds of them myself. She went on. "And your pigeon is so whiney. He doesn't do anything." That puzzled me, because the pigeon did hitch a ride on that yacht. She didn't say a word about the clam, and I'd thought that was the best part. She said other things, but I don't believe I heard them because I was so devastated. I couldn't believe it. Neither could Rosemary, but she simply shrugged and said, "I have dozens of my own manuscripts in the closet."

Dozens? I didn't have any, except the pigeon one. It was clear the editor thought it was dreadful, and though she'd told me why, I didn't understand her reasons and had no idea of how to fix it. Of course I'd expected to succeed on my first try: that happens all the time in the movies. The thought of having dozens of unsold manuscripts stuffed into a closet was appalling. Surely I wouldn't have to go through all those false starts. Nonetheless, *The Pigeon Who Wanted To Be a Seagull* became the first of my many manuscripts that ended up where the sun never shines.

I don't know whether to be embarrassed or proud of the fact that I had committed all the classic errors novice writers for children make. I'd bet my last cup of cold coffee that among the readers of this chapter are enough red faces to heat a small publishing house. I've seen your manuscripts: the one about the chicken that hoped to find happiness at Kentucky Fried, the triangle that wanted to be a square, the skinny bear that tried to gain weight by growing candy bars. We've all done it, and now that we've confessed, we can go on to improve our ways.

This is the first secret of the slush pile: a high percentage of the manuscripts that turn up there are as dreadful as mine was. They come with letters that read:

"I've never written a children's book before."

"My grandchildren have always loved this story."

"Kindly note that this material is copyrighted."

Sometimes the stationery has birds and flowers on it, and sometimes it has a letterhead with a name followed by the word "writer." If you are guilty of any of the above, you should know another secret: They tip off whoever is opening the mail that she's got another one from an amateur. A glance at page one, and the ms. is ready to go back to the writer. Are we heartless? No, we are fighting for self-preservation because the average publishing house receives three to five thousand manuscripts a year.

Of these about 80 percent come from people who not only have never written a children's book but seem never to have read one. Many submissions are illiterate, amateurish, old-fashioned—and even meant for adults. We once received an ad for boots with a request to send a pair in size seven. (We still wonder if some shoe-store published the manuscript. We didn't send the boots.) Far too many people entertain romantic ideas of being published and have no idea what writing a book entails. They write down the first thing that enters their minds and send it off to publishers. Most will not make it past the first reader because the writer is working out a fantasy and has no desire to do the work real writers do. It is because of the flood of this kind of material that editors call unsolicited manuscripts slush.

Marilyn Marlow of Curtis Brown once chided me for calling it that. "We like to think of it as the discovery pile," she said. I try to think of it that way, too, because we do receive material from writers who are serious about their work and look at each submission that has made it past the first reader with anticipation. Will this one be publishable? Or, is this a writer to be encouraged to try again? We want to publish you, but you have to be ready.

Different houses have different systems, but usually the slush pile is allocated to one person whose duty it is to log in the manuscript by date, title, and author. Sometimes an acknowledgment is sent, but not always. This person will then either read it herself or pass it on to another assistant, depending on the subject matter. This is called the first reading.

The assistant, who joined the firm with the certainty that she would find the next Judy Blume (originally a slush pile author) in the "discovery pile," has by now become jaded. She knows that stories written in verse are usually bad, and has become prejudiced against them. She feels the same way about books with talking animals, insects, or machines. Still, she tries to be fair and will read a page or two of a picture book manuscript, and maybe ten to twenty pages of a novel. Because of her experience, she can tell quickly whether a manuscript has promise, and soon clears her desk of most of the unsolicited material.

What about the remaining 20 percent? She comes across a thoughtful treatment of a nonfiction subject—but her house publishes no nonfiction. Yet another picture book manuscript—but her house publishes only one or two picture books a year, and by the same artists and writers each time. Here's a well-written novel—but her house published a novel on a similar subject just a year ago. So another 5 percent are returned to their authors, not because of poor quality, but "because they're not right for the list," that catch-all phrase publishers use so often. These returns are not caused by lack of artistry but by failure on the writer's part to research the particular needs of each publishing house or by circumstances beyond the writer's control. And that's another secret: being declined by one house does not mean you shouldn't send the manuscript elsewhere.

Twenty-six editors declined Madeleine L'Engle's *A Wrinkle in Time*; then one who appreciated fantasy bought the book. Editors are not perfect; each of us has in her past at least one book we turned down that went on to become a best-seller or prizewinner.

And now for the final 15 percent, written by people who are serious writers, who have done their homework, including keeping up with the latest books via publisher's catalogs, children's book media, and regular trips to the children's rooms of their local libraries and bookstores. Often these last books are nicely written but with nothing outstanding about them, or are books that almost make it but are too slight, as an editorial note to the writer might say. Or a fantasy may start out with an interesting premise and then get mired down in murkiness and logorrhea (so many fantasies are just too long!) because the writer has lost control of his material. Still, a manuscript like this shows promise in the first few chapters, so the assistant reads the whole thing, hoping it may be publishable.

Another secret of the slush pile is that the assistants want to find publishable material. I've known first readers to rush in to me with a manuscript because, compared with all the dross, this one was real: neatly typed, well-written, interesting, and with good grammar and spelling. Manuscripts like this always stand a chance.

Some editors, who see about 2 or 3 percent of the unsolicited manuscripts after the assistant has passed them on for a second reading, will seriously ponder a few promising manuscripts and may work hard and closely with the writer to make them publishable. Another editor may return a manuscript with a few comments, to help the writer see some of the problems. But because she already has too many commitments she cannot take on a problem-laden piece of work from a beginner and does not want to see the material again. Yet another editor may be seriously interested in the work; he may write an encouraging letter suggesting revisions, ending with the hope that the writer will send it in again once revised.

Unfortunately, editors are not always clear about whether they wish to see manuscripts again. The writer may wonder whether she should work on it along the lines of the suggestions and resubmit it, or whether she should revise and send the manuscript elsewhere. If an editor has taken the time to give a manuscript a thoughtful reading and to express his feelings about it, it's as good a sign as any that he'd like to see it again. It certainly won't hurt to send it back, so don't be shy: the worst that can happen is that the manuscript will be declined again.

Another secret of the slush pile is that even if *every* unsolicited manuscript were a potential Newbery-winner, no publisher could accommodate them all. Publishing houses have limits on the number of titles they can publish in a given year; these are usually set by the financial people, not the editors. Most of the scheduled books are from writers in the publisher's regular stable, many of whom write a book a year. If an editor is to buy a book from a new writer, she has to feel it's outstanding, unique, so well-written that she's got to publish it. Sorry to say, but of the thousands of manuscripts in the slush pile this may happen only once a year—or not at all. But it does happen, so don't lose heart.

The situation is not so competitive at houses with longer lists or at new houses without a stable—and that's where a new writer stands the best chance. Another secret of the slush pile is that the writer who keeps up with the staff changes in publishing houses has an edge. When an editor leaves her old house to take up an editorship elsewhere, she will have left many of her authors behind and will be actively seeking ones for her new list. This is one advantage of having an agent: he knows who's who and where they are and what's being looked for. It's more difficult for a writer to keep up with staff changes, but it's not impossible. Most writers' organizations and media stay current with the movements of editors and changes in the market, so a membership in a group like the Society of Children's Book Writers (SCBW) or a subscription to a writers' magazine is a definite asset.

This is no secret, but sometimes it seems as if it is, because time after time a manuscript is returned to the writer simply because he sent it to the wrong place, wasting postage and time. Where should you send the manuscript, assuming you don't have an agent? No one else knows the work as well as you do, so with this in mind, begin your research at your local library.

It is hard to find a town so small, so isolated that a library is not nearby, which, when you think about it, is a boon we take for granted. Inside, there's a librarian who should have a copy of *The Literary Marketplace* at the reference desk or be able to get you one by interlibrary loan. This annual is the publishing bible, and carries lists of the major publishers by name and region as well as the names of editors, agents, writers' organizations, and anything germane to the business. If you find the pages and pages of publishers too daunting to work from, and if your car is parked in a one-hour zone, you might find it easier to look into some of the magazines that deal with children's books. Important ones are *School Library Journal, Booklist, The Horn Book*—which review books for all ages— and *VOYA* (*Voice of Youth Advocates*)—which reviews books for teenagers, or young adult books. A good librarian will be able to steer you toward others.

If you can't find a helpful library, you can obtain a list of children's book publishers from SCBW, if you are a member, in return for a self-addressed stamped envelope (SASE). The Children's Book Council in New York will also send you on request their "Members' List" of publishers, editors, and art directors, and "Members' Publishing Programs," containing brief descriptions of various publishers' list.

Another resource is free publishers' catalogs, which you may obtain by sending a SASE with your request to the children's marketing departments. However, it's been my experience that you won't hear from all of them, so don't let this be your sole resort. You can also try bookstores, which may have extra catalogs, and you can definitely pick up publishers' catalogs at the many writers' and librarians' conferences around the country. A catalog can be extremely useful to the writer, since it lists all the books in print at that house along with future titles. In addition to discovering who publishes which author or what kind of book, you'll also get an idea of where the kind of book you write is likeliest to find a home.

If you wish to know whether an idea for a nonfiction book you are contemplating has been published recently, go back to the reference library and look up the topic in *Children's Books in Print*, which lists books by title, author, and subject; don't forget the library card catalog. It may be that there hasn't been a book on your subject for a number of years, so an up-to-date one will be welcome.

Once you've become familiar with these sources, you'll be able to relax, but you should make an effort twice a year to get your hands on the *Publishers Weekly* (*PW*) spring and fall children's book announcement issues. You can order them directly from *PW* or you may find these special issues at a bookstore. Nearly all the major children's publishers take out list ads in the announcement issues, and you can see at a glance what's being published and learn about upcoming books in advance. Not too long ago, an illustrator whom I met at a writers' conference told me about a picture book she was working on. "Whoops," I said. "Simon & Schuster is publishing a picture book with the same idea next month!" "I'll have to get a copy," she said, "and make sure mine is different." If you can afford it, consider subscribing to *PW*, since it covers children's books every week. *PW* is the most current source of information about the publishing industry. It carries ads, reviews, interviews with writers, personnel changes, and much more.

Magazines like *The Writer* and *Writer's Digest* can also be useful, but the most important periodical for the writer of children's books is the SCBW *Bulletin*, available through membership in the Society. In addition to news articles, the *Bulletin* contains marketing information for manuscripts and lists conferences of special interest. If this last came as a surprise to you, I strongly recommend that you join SCBW. It is the only organization exclusively dedicated to helping the writer of children's books, and its membership is growing: you'll be at a disadvantage if you're not a member.

It may be that you're already familiar with all this material and no longer entertain fantasies about an immediate, enthusiastic acceptance. You're aware that editorial staffs are underpaid and overworked, and you know that a silence of two months means nothing either way about the fate of your book. Is there anything else you can do, assuming you've written a book that is competitive with what is being published? How can you make an editor pay attention?

Your original manuscript looks inviting, neatly typed (double-spaced, on white 8 ½ × 11 bond) with a good, dark ribbon. If you used a word processor, you avoided the fonts that look like computer print, chose one that resembles typewriter type—like 12-point Courier—and printed the manuscript without justifying the margins, because justifying leaves big spaces within the lines and makes the manuscript harder to read. You also have kept a clearly reproduced, legible copy of the manuscript. The title is clever—your son helped you with it—and it should appeal to kids. Your local librarian or bookseller agreed with you that the idea was timely and one children would be interested in. You're not using the Snoopy notepaper for cover letters any longer, and you decided not to add the word "writer" or your photograph to the letterhead you ordered from your local printer: it has just your name, address, and telephone number on it. Is there anything more you can do?

How about that cover letter? Editors are busy people (or so you keep hearing) and don't relish two or three single-spaced pages of self-praise or synopsis. Even though you've never published a children's book before, you don't announce it right off. You don't even mention the fact, but you do say you have been writing for a number of years and have published stories in children's magazines (if that's true). If you have no credentials, your letter is short and simple and thanks the editor for taking the time to consider it. Be positive about yourself and whatever you've done.

But here's another slush pile secret, one that can lift your letter over all the others. Why not find out something about the editor and compliment her? Perhaps you agree with a comment she made that was quoted in *PW*. Maybe one of her books won a major award recently. If you know nothing about the person, you can at least say that the list is impressive with many titles that caught your attention and which you're looking forward to reading. A genuine compliment conveys your professionalism to the reader of the letter. It'll be clear you're not playing Russian roulette with publishers, and perhaps your friendly tone will result in a friendly answer.

Ms. Annabelle Jones, Editor
Bench Press
123 Fourth Street
New York, NY 10000

Dear Ms. Jones:

I heard you speak at the New Jersey conference last month and found your talk informative and lively. I was especially pleased to hear that you were looking for humorous novels for ages 10–14, and I hope you find the enclosed manuscript for EATING DOGFOOD IS NO FUN right for your list.

It is about Jennifer, whose family is divorcing, which has caused her younger brother, Elvis, to run away from home. During Jennifer's search for Elvis she teams up with Rodney, a boy from her school, and they become friends. The book is set in a small town near a summer resort, and although the subject has its serious side, I hope the reader will find it amusing as well.

Thank you for considering my work.

Sincerely,

Cover letter finished, it's time to put it and a copy of the manuscript into a stiff folder or box to protect it from creasing. Then slide it into a manila envelope or padded mailbag with your SASE.

Please consider the person who will open that envelope, and seal it carefully but not so tightly that it will take a machete to open it.

Now to the post office, fingers crossed. The clerk will help you decide how to send the manuscript; you may wish to pay extra for a return receipt, or you may have had the foresight to include a stamped, self-addressed postcard that the publisher can return to you upon receipt. It is a waste of money to pay for Express Mail or Priority Service; simple first- or fourth-class works fine.

A long wait is ahead of you, so begin your next book. If you're a writer, you write. Let others just wait. You know better than to haunt the mailbox because if you haven't heard within two months, you're going to write the editor a friendly note (do *not* telephone), asking whether she's made a decision. And if you don't hear within thirty days after that, you're going to write again, stating that you are withdrawing the manuscript from consideration and wish it returned. Three months with *no word of any kind* is quite enough time to wait, and the lack of a response may well be a sign of a lack of interest. You don't want to deliver an ultimatum or put pressure on an overworked staff, but neither do you have time to waste. Of course, if they say the manuscript is having a second reading or they'd like more time with it, you'll grant them another month or two before you write again. (Yes, they'll resent it when you remind them again, but don't you resent waiting forever?) If you've heard nothing from them, and even if your manuscript is not returned, make another copy and submit it elsewhere. This procedure is fair to you and the editor and is the one the SCBW recommends to its members.

Many editors have said they don't mind multiple submissions of manuscripts; you can find out who they are from your market research. Susan Hirschmann of Greenwillow has even said that "Anyone who doesn't multiple submit is crazy—it just takes too long." Random House and others disagree, and will state that it is against their policy to consider multiple submissions. Why?

Maybe you'll be lucky and only one publisher out of the five to whom you send the manuscript will write back expressing interest. But suppose two (or more) publishers want to buy your work, leaving you with an embarrassing choice—and confession—to make. You could avoid embarrassment by stating in your cover letter that you're making a multiple submission, although many writers do not.

Far more serious than embarrassment is the possibility that a flood of multiple submissions may eventually cause more publishers to declare permanent moratoriums on reading unsolicited manuscripts. If one third of the manuscripts in my office are multiple submissions, then my workload has increased. Publishers simply do not have enough staff to handle the amount of material that comes in.

Writers are quick to blame editors, but editors know the problem lies in the vast amount of dreadful material that comes in, coupled with the lack of in-house readers. When I was first in publishing, houses had full-time readers who spent all their time logging in and reading submissions. I came across an old log from the 1940s once. Each book had a four-by-six-inch file card, with title, author, names of readers, opinions, etc. I doubt that anyone is that meticulous today; on the contrary, some houses don't even bother to log the manuscripts, pleading lack of staff time. Publishers have done away with readers, so the burden falls on assistants, who are secretaries and factotums—and editors, who, much as they would love to, have almost no time during the workday to read anything, let alone unsolicited manuscripts coming in at the rate of a hundred a month or more (of which an estimated thirty-five are multiple submissions).

All of us have been hurt by the multiple-submission practice. Imagine this scenario. Annabelle finally reads your manuscript, which her assistant has passed on; it had been in the house six months. She loves it! She calls you. "Sorry," you say, "I sold it to Peachfuzz Press two weeks ago." It doesn't matter to you now, but five or ten precious hours of two persons' worktime, which could have been spent on a manuscript that had not been multiple-submitted, have flown out the window. Another author has to wait longer because you took time away from at least two busy editors and their staffs. The reason you had to wait six months was because other writers had multiple-submitted ahead of you. It's a vicious circle, and not good for the morale of either the writer or the editor.

Most editors, agents, and the SCBW believe it's still best to send a manuscript to one publisher at a time. They also advise writers not to send more than one manuscript to each publisher at one time. Waiting may be frustrating, but in the long run this procedure will work out for the best. But that's what editors usually say, and you're impatient. What to do?

You could join a writers' organization and begin a campaign to approach publishers with complaints about the turnaround time for manuscripts, pleading that more staff be hired. While you're waiting for results, also try the following:

Send query letters with sample chapters and an outline for a nonfiction book to several publishers at once; that's a shortcut, often, and doesn't take too much time out of anyone's day. (Do not query editors about short works such as picture books, storybooks, or easy readers; you must submit the entire manuscript for these.) Many editors prefer to read a few chapters and an outline for a nonfiction book and will let you know whether they're interested in seeing more. This procedure is fine for nonfiction, but I believe it's wrong for novels, with the exception of paperback series, since, as Michelle Poploff of Dell says, "Many times we work with concepts, a word or two with which young readers can immediately identify, such as Pen Pals or Creepy Creatures." If editors decide that a concept is weak, then you'll have been saved a great deal of work.

But at a traditional hardcover house, you are not competing with others' *ideas* for books. You have written a novel. The best part might be in the middle, and your beginning might be slow—do you want your book judged on what might be its weakest section? Also, an editor who's read three promising chapters and has asked to see more may not be so enthusiastic about the book the second time around; his initial excitement has had time to diminish during the wait, and other projects have come along to take up his attention. Some editors say that a few chapters are enough for them, but I think it's foolish to give this kind of preview, as if your work were a TV movie. Remember, you are trying to sell a *novel*, a long, coherent work, not a fragment. You are shortchanging yourself and your work by not letting the whole book speak for itself.

You may have heard that a cover letter is not necessary. It isn't. All material is looked at, with or without a cover letter. But a cover letter can work for you as an introduction, and good manners lead to people feeling better disposed toward each other. A manuscript without a cover letter is like food dumped on the table. It may be edible, but it's not inviting. On those days when I feel especially frazzled, I'm tempted to return the manuscript without reading it and without even a form letter, as if it were from Nobody to Nobody.

Another custom that has an adverse psychological effect is the practice, since the advent of word processors, of writers to say in their cover letters, "If you're not interested in my manuscript, don't return it—discard it." Postage is expensive, but I can't help feeling that the writer doesn't respect his work if he can so cavalierly say "toss it out." As a consequence, I find it hard to respect it too, since even if I owned stock in Xerox and IBM, I wouldn't want my precious words filling wastebaskets all over the country. And what about the sheer waste of trees?

Not too long ago, a colleague stormed into my office, waving some papers. "Someone just faxed me a proposal," she cried. "It's going straight into the wastebasket. How dare they tie up our fax line!" Most editors feel the same way, so don't even think about faxing unsolicited material to a publisher.

Civility will not guarantee publication, but it will make the search less stressful for all concerned. Learn to accept an editor's declining (we never "reject") your manuscript with equanimity, and send it out again. Or you could take Kin Platt's approach. He, who has many books to his credit, told me that when one of his manuscripts is declined, he tells himself "The editor is an idiot," and sends it out again. (Note he does not tell the editor she is an idiot!) "A writer has to have a strong ego," he says. If you have faith in your talent, you must believe that an editor will one day respond favorably to it, so keep trying.

Even though I knew much of this way back when I bumbled into that editor's office with *The Pigeon Who Wanted To Be a Seagull*, I ignored it. I truly felt my book was wonderful and worth publishing. You may think I had an advantage in being able to walk into an editor's office and ask her opinion, but this opportunity turned into disaster for me. It's one thing to get an impersonal note declining your manuscript because "it's not suitable"; it's quite another to be told face-to-face that it's trite, derivative, and boring. It took me ten years to recover from that blow, to gain the confidence to try writing again, and to understand what she meant by "passive hero" (a term I'll explain later). She was correct in her evaluation of my manuscript—I can appreciate that now—but I was naïvely looking for special treatment.

As one hopeful writer told me, "I can pick out simple tunes on the piano, but learning to read music and how to play chords will take effort. After that I must learn technique and expression. And I must practice and practice. The analogy holds true for writing."

I didn't think of writing in that way when I wrote my pigeon story, and that's why it never got off the ground. But if you keep learning, practicing, and persisting, you will be published. Take the risk. You'll live through the rejections. You'll never win if you don't begin.

2 What Do Editors Want?

THE SUCCESSFUL WRITER has to understand what an editor wants. Of course an editor wants good books, but beyond that an editor wants good books that sell well. If you understand the current state of juvenile publishing and the market, you are ahead of the crowd. First, a bit of history, which may help.

For as long as I can remember juvenile publishing has been like a cottage industry. Small departments, tucked far away from adult books, as if they might contaminate the loftier reaches, worked autonomously and inconspicuously under great editors—from May Massee at Viking to Ursula Nordstrom at Harper—and produced one fine book after another.

Even today, individual juvenile departments are run in the same way under the direction of an editor-in-chief who passed through a long apprenticeship and is committed to continuing with the great tradition of the past. History will tell us which of today's editors is great, but so will a walk around a major conference. The good books are still being published, and I trust they always will be.

But fateful changes have taken place, beginning in the 1960s, when many publishers were either merged with other ones in huge conglomerates or bought by major corporations. By the end of the 1980s, it seemed as if all the publishers were huddling under only half a dozen corporate umbrellas, and the day was not far off when only one colossal publisher, with a zillion imprints, would be left.

In addition, since the mid seventies the most successful children's trade publishers have been publishing for bookstores, including the chains like Walden and B. Dalton's, as well as for the traditional school and library—the institutional—markets. The

1980s saw this trend come into full flower. Children's publishers had long flourished by supplying books to libraries—at one point over 90 percent of sales were to the institutional market—but the 1970s saw the public libraries decreasing their hours (a trend that is still continuing) or even closing their doors. Even today, many are finding their purchasing budgets reduced or eliminated. Three of the biggest library markets in the United States suffered severe cost-cutting beginning in the 1970s: New York, California, and Texas.

It is, then, a tribute to their intelligence, imagination, and resilience that children's book editors were able to adapt to the changing marketplace by publishing books that would have sales in bookstores. These were often books that libraries had frowned upon, such as pop-ups and series. Children's paperbacks led the way in the bookstores, and it was the money received from paperback houses for paperback reprint rights that kept more than one traditional hardcover house afloat.

We've come through the economic hard times of the seventies, when publishers were laying off children's book people and cutting back on the number of titles published—it was a difficult time for a writer to get started. And now we've sailed through the experimental days of the eighties, which saw the rise of "commercial" books, packagers, and series publishing, where it seemed the literary book didn't have a chance—and it often didn't. On the other hand, writers who had been writing for children rather than for librarians and reviewers came into their own.

Bookstores, like publishers, must be profitable if they are to survive. The chain stores in the malls pulled in the kids who just had to have number 99 of the latest Sweet Valley–Horror–Pen-Pal–Babysitter book. Bantam's Choose Your Own Adventure series sold over thirty million copies in 10 years—and, more important, pulled boys as well as girls into reading books. Girls bought over fifty million Sweet Valley books. The chains had learned a profitable lesson: children and teenagers *will* spend their own money on books.

Fortunately for those of us who love good books, the chains, which operate by guessing what customers want, are not the only ships on the sea. Independent booksellers—the so-called mom-and-pop stores—found themselves filling in the quality gap at the chains and helped hardcovers become best-sellers, too. A record number of privately owned children's bookstores opened for business in the 1980s, and the children's departments in general bookstores expanded. Before this explosion bookstores devoted only 5 to 10 percent of the shelves to children's books. Being an independent bookseller was no longer the fastest way to bankruptcy, as it had been in the 1970s.

The main reason for this record expansion of sales of children's books is a simple one: more children are being born. Schools are crowded with mini–baby-boomers, and baby carriages are everywhere. I rejoice every time I see one! Many are yuppies' kids, whose parents have already registered them for college, and are teaching them to read in the crib. All parents who care about their children's minds are turning toward books and away from TV and the VCR and movies that offer simply too much junk. Some communities are even providing special "enrichment" classes in an effort to provide an alternative to Saturday morning TV. You don't have to be rich to enjoy books: the library is free, paperbacks are cheap, and hardcovers are affordable for the many two-paycheck couples with high-level jobs. In short, parents and children are in the bookstores, buying. They are also in the libraries.

Coinciding with the baby boom was the merger-mania of the eighties when MBAs discovered, as ever more corporations gobbled up publishing houses, that children's books meant business. While profits sagged on the adult side of trade publishing, they were soaring on the children's side. This has resulted in a demand for more titles: nearly five thousand books for children were published in 1990.

To make a good thing even better, educators, dismayed by the low reading scores among American children, decided it was time to throw out the basal readers and replace them with trade books, in the belief that children would learn eagerly if the reading was interesting. Basal readers were noted for their blandness, as you may remember from your own school days. The "whole language" program began in New Zealand, for use with Maori children. In the United States, California led the way, and the movement also became known as the California Reading Initiative. Other states soon followed. This, then, led to yet another demand for new children's books.

Not since the 1960s, the halcyon days of Title II, when the government was subsidizing libraries, has the writer had such an opportunity to break into the children's book field. In the 1960s, publishers turned out books for the library market in record numbers. Not all those books were wonderful, but they were of higher quality on average, since they had to pass muster among the librarians. Today, the bookstore market is child-oriented, but giving kids what they want is not always giving them the best. The school and library market also wants books that children will enjoy reading, but it has higher literary standards when it comes to choosing books for schoolchildren.

The trends for the nineties are in place. Even the government has announced a concern about the educational performance of American children. As a consequence, we are going back to the traditional mix of books for young people that prevailed in the past, with a few twists. Publishers are watching the demographics, and the writer should, too. The mini–baby boom began in the late seventies, when the oldest baby boomers were beginning to worry about their biological clocks; it has been peaking ever since. Writers should pay attention to their local schools. Which class needs the most space? The fourth graders? What about the sophomores in high school? Are they complaining about overcrowding? It wasn't so long ago that schools were closing down; right now they're expanding.

Like all who are concerned about the cultural and intellectual welfare of young people, most juvenile editors feel that the nineties marks a threshold of hope, our last chance for not only peace but for the solution of the many social problems afflicting our society: Drug addiction, AIDS, homelessness, pollution, the erosion of Constitutional rights, the backlash aimed at the hard-won battles of the sixties and seventies, bank failures, selfishness and corruption in high places (we've always had that, but never before have we so admired it!), the worship of image over substance, the selling of everything, including war.

Calvin Coolidge said that the business of America was business—and not since the twenties has this idea run so rampant. The American language is full of phrases referring to money: "Will they buy that idea?" "It pays to read good books." "Can you sell him on that?" We deplore the fact that books are called product, singular, as if all books were as equal as bags of sugar. Yet editors today have "bought into" the fact that the bottom line has to look good if we are to continue publishing books. We are, therefore, open to "commercial" books as well as "literary" books, and we dream of finding that marvel, the good book that sells well.

To sell well, a book has to appeal to today's children. And we must have a clear idea of what modern children are like. In many ways they are not so different from the way we once were, but they lose their innocence at a younger age than we did—this has been true for the last twenty years or so. Today's readers are children with a veneer of false sophistication. They have been exposed to some of the outward manifestations of adulthood—violence, sex, drugs, broken families—without having acquired the maturity to deal with such issues. But make no mistake, they are planning ahead. Some are wise and some are not, and some confuse street lore with knowledge. They need help from their elders, who are the last people they want to ask for it.

Those of us who write or publish books for children have a unique chance to reach these young people. Books remain a private endeavor for kids, especially if they are free to buy the books of their choice. What are we going to teach these kids while we entertain them? And how will we entertain them while we teach them? Children enjoy learning new things, and isn't it sad that so many people say school is boring! Learning something new—no matter how difficult it may be—is exciting because it instills a sense of accomplishment. One heartening study found that children age three to eight preferred to watch public TV instead of network pap. The challenge to today's writers is to reach these children, to inform without being dull or didactic.

The writer has greater freedom than ever because a wide range of young readers is waiting for his books. With the concern about education, he can write nonfiction for the school library market. Or because of the paperback market he can specialize in action-packed series for the mass-market houses and chain bookstores. Or he can write picture books, storybooks, "chapter books," novels for ages nine to thirteen and young adult books for teenage readers.

But if diversity is the keynote, how can a writer keep up with the marketplace? For one thing it's a mistake to write for a "market," switching from trend to trend, and finding you were a little too early or a little too late. From the time you get an idea to the time the book is published may take three years or longer, by which time a fad is over. A writer should be aware of what's in the stores and libraries—it's so easy to be considered "old-fashioned" by kids—but he should stick to what he's most comfortable with.

The Swiss psychologist Jean Piaget said that children grow intellectually in a sequence, as their minds grow, step by step. Between the ages of two and six, children are limited in their thinking because they tend to focus on only one aspect of experience, and they are extremely egocentric. When they are about six or seven, children begin to see the interrelationship between ideas and experience. By the time they are twelve, they are able to understand the relationship between their image of the world and a more general and abstract view. The kinds of books they like to read mirror their mental and social development at each developmental stage.

The traditional mix of children's books includes material for the preschool child, such as pop-up or movable books, board books, fold-in or flap books, and books that are almost toys. Even before they can read, children will pick up novelty books and turn the pages as if they were reading.

However, it is difficult for a writer to enter the novelty book market. An illustrator has a better chance, and a packager the best chance of all. Novelty books have special production requirements. For example, the concept may require that the book take a special shape or have a hole in the middle of the paper. Lois Ehlert's Caldecott Honor Book, *Color Zoo*, is an example of a die-cut book. It is also a nonfiction book, since its purpose is to teach elementary ideas, in this case, colors and shapes. Many preschool books teach simple concepts such as the alphabet, numbers, and animal behavior (e.g., birds live in nests). Some of these are board books, with pages made of glossy cardboard for sturdiness. Or they may be touch-and-feel like *Pat the Bunny*. Publishers use nontoxic inks and papers on books for infants and toddlers, since they often end up in children's mouths. The Chubby Board Books have padded covers, and some books for babies are made of cloth. There are even plastic ones that float in the tub. As a rule, libraries prefer not to stock novelty books because, with their specially cut paper and movable parts, they are often too fragile for general circulation.

Ideas are cheap, but execution is expensive, and this is especially true of novelty books. A few publishers have production departments that can handle the paper engineering and other special requirements of novelty books, or they may hire consultants. Others, who may do only one or two a year, will buy the books from packagers and foreign publishers. On occasion a writer or illustrator will propose a concept, as Rosemary Wells did with her Max board books, which so delights an editor that she will take it on. But this is rare: most concepts come from editors and are assigned to artists they work with regularly. Some packagers are receptive to ideas from outside writers, but originality and appeal have to be strong.

If you want to succeed in this market you have to be more than a writer or illustrator. You must make a full-time commitment to this genre, as Harriet Ziefert has done. A former teacher, she understands the concepts children need and like, and has built up ties with artists and printers, so that she can package and sell her ideas. She will bring working dummies and art samples to editors to illustrate the concept. She will also arrange for the manufacture of them. Intervisual of California works the same way, as do Zokeisha and others. You can obtain a list of children's book packagers and other information from the American Book Producers Association, an international trade organization of independent packagers in the United States and Canada.

When the child is able to comprehend a story—the ages vary, but can be as young as two—parents read aloud from trade picture books and storybooks. A picture book is mostly pictures; a storybook is mostly words, but has many pictures. Pre-school children adore silly cumulative stories, scary stories, and stories about disobedience (all of which are found in a traditional tale like *The Gingerbread Boy*) as well as gentle books about nature, like *Blueberries for Sal*, by Robert McCloskey. A current trend is to break long stories into chapters, but they are not true "chapter books," which are short novels.

Around the end of second grade, many children spurn the heavily illustrated picture books ("baby books," they call them), and look for what they call "chapter books." Finally, the child can read on her own, and publishers provide easy-to-read books that invite her to read with a simple vocabulary, short sentences, and lots of white space. If the book is broken into chapters, the child feels she's reading a "grown-up" book. Whether in the form of a storybook or novel, chapter books are an excellent medium for tall tales as well as contemporary, realistic stories. Humor is particularly popular.

Patricia Reilly Giff's series, the Kids of the Polk Street School, is one of the most successful examples of short novels for young readers. Although Giff wrote them for the second-grade reading level, fifth graders enjoy them, too—especially if they are reluctant readers. The many fantasy adventures of Pippi Longstocking, by Astrid Lindgren, also fit perfectly into this category, for a slightly older or better reader, from ages eight to eleven. Books about family life, school, friendship, and summer vacations, especially those told with humor, appeal to children in this age group. Writers like Robert Burch, Louis Sachar, and Beverly Cleary excel in writing books for this age. Eight- or nine-year-olds crave independence but know they're not quite ready for it: however, they're all set to explore the world through books.

Middle-age readers, nine- to thirteen-year-olds, can handle any subject, and they're ready for more depth in their reading. Many of the children's classics seem meant for this age, from *Rebecca of Sunnybrook Farm* to *Summer of the Swans* and *A Wrinkle in Time*. In a lighter vein, Paula Danziger, usually regarded as a young adult novelist, finds many readers among ten-year-olds!

So many writers have written such marvelous books for this age group that it would take me hours to list them, but preeminent among our contemporaries are Joan Aiken, Betsy Byars, Judy Blume, James Lincoln Collier and Christopher Collier, Paula Fox, Susan Cooper, Lois Lowry, Patricia MacLachlan, Robin McKinley, Katherine Paterson, Richard Peck, E. L. Konigsburg, Zilpha Keatley Snyder, Jerry Spinelli, Virginia Hamilton, Leon Garfield, Vivien Alcock, Rosa Guy, Diana Wynne-Jones, Walter Dean Myers—and all your own personal favorites.

Middle-grade fiction is not all fun and games, and writers can deal with real problems—a twelve-year-old alcoholic is different from one who's sixteen, for example, and drug dealers are hanging around grammar schools. But if you want to tackle a contemporary problem like child abuse, be aware that a great many books on that subject have already been published, and yours has to be outstanding. The trouble with most "problem" novels is that they are dreary and revolve around the "problem"—when real life is more interesting and complex.

You don't have to be a psychologist to understand children. A friend wrote me the following about her just-turned-twelve daughter:

> At the moment, Julia prefers mystery/thriller books, but also very much likes mythological stories. *Daughter of Earth* [the

picture book by Gerald McDermott] is still one of her favorites, and she has a keen interest in Indian lore. She also likes fictionalized anthropology and has read the *Clan of the Cave Bear* series several times. . . . She is quite mature for her age, yet in so many ways, as I see it, she really is only a child still.

Middle-grade fiction is perhaps the most satisfying category for a writer. Children are still children, but their curiosity is unbounded, and the writer who can enthrall them will be cherished. Statistics have shown that this age is also known for having the most readers as a group. To satisfy these voracious and varied readers, think about writing thrillers, literary novels, fantasy and science fiction, gripping historical fiction, humor, and books about contemporary problems from the greenhouse effect to the effects of gossip. We desperately need fresh approaches to problems, and at the middle-grade level, we must convey a sense of optimism about life. Robert Cormier's *The Chocolate War* is not intended for ten-year-olds, but they would enjoy his book, *Other Bells To Ring*, about a twelve-year-old girl's interest in Catholicism.

The young adult market, twelve-to-sixteen-year-olds, has gone through many changes. Thirty years ago, YA was a librarian's classification for adult books that were suitable for young people. The most famous of these is probably *The Catcher in the Rye* by J. D. Salinger, a book about a teenage boy that was originally written for adults. Some critics contend that *Catcher in the Rye* gave birth to the YA market: serious, literary books written especially for teenagers.

Today, however, some publishers are dividing the YA market into three types: the young YA, which is read by ten-year-olds eager to be teenagers (Paula Danziger); the middle YA, about teen life (Richard Peck); and the mature YA, written about mature issues (Robert Cormier). The YA writer is competing with writers for adults, like Stephen King, and has to find a way to reach teenagers. Paula Danziger is famous for her quirky titles, Peck likes to throw in a disaster with some gore, and Cormier pulls no punches in writing about sex or violence.

Writers and editors have to think like marketing people and come up with a "handle," a one-sentence (or less) description of a book that tells the prospective reader what is in store for him—and makes him want to read it. For example, "While their father is away at war, four girls learn about life and love" (*Little Women*) or "The long search for her runaway brother helps Jennifer reconcile her parents, who want to divorce" (*Eating Dogfood Is No Fun*). Sometimes the handle comes to the writer before he starts writing; other times it will come when he's finished. If you cannot reduce your book to one sentence, then it's too complex and unfocused, and you need to ask yourself, "What is my book about?" The well-baited hook will land the reading fish.

Publishers are interested in a full range of books, and the writer can find her own niche without worrying about trends. In 1950 Frances Clarke Sayers wrote, "It is imperative that the writer for children be close to his own childhood." The writer must also study children today. A thirty-seven-year-old mother and writer recently told me, "Life has changed so much for kids since I grew up. I've got to write about it. They need me." Merge your past with the present, write with feeling, and do the best you can. Somewhere out there an editor is waiting for your book.

3 The Perils of the Picture Book

OST PEOPLE THINK of picture books when they hear the words "children's books." And most beginning writers think the same. The slush piles at the publishing houses contain more picture book manuscripts (ten to one, it seems) than any other kind. Picture books appeal to everyone. They're short, tell a simple story, and have marvelous illustrations. It is precisely for these reasons that they are difficult to carry off.

Ruth Cantor, the literary agent, has said that she does not want to look at picture book manuscripts any longer. "My mail is flooded with them, and most are dreadful," she told me. She's right, and some publishers refuse to read them, too, for the same reasons. Most of the manuscripts in the picture book slush pile are anthropomorphic, condescending, derivative, didactic, sentimental, or have passive protagonists. If you're guilty of any of these charges, you will not be published (unless you're a celebrity).

Where do all these poor manuscripts come from? From amateurs. People who think "cute" animals and a simple-minded (condescending) or saccharine (sentimental) story are all it takes to appeal to a little boy or girl: the majority of submissions are about animals, though we do get our fair share of manuscripts about talking machines, clouds, and even molecules (anthropomorphic). Some stories are about children, often the story of a child who misbehaves and is punished (didactic). One particularly grisly one was about a boy who refused to cut his toenails, and ended up kidnapped into forced labor as punishment.

Most of these writers probably haven't read a recent children's book. Possibly they've looked at some titles in the bookstore and, with the memory of books they read as children, sit down and write. The resulting stories are usually patterned on what they've read or seen in the movies or on TV. The next step is to read the story to a child. When they submit the manuscript, they tell the editor the book is "child-tested." It's a rare child who doesn't like being read to while held on a lap, so the testing is not exactly un-biased. Nor is it necessary. If anything, the child-tested claim alien-ates the editor. Most annoying are the cover letters that tell us the manuscript is just right for a certain market, as if we didn't know what the markets were!

Any editor or assistant worth her salt has a "child" inside her, the one she used to be. When she reads a submission, the inner child reads along with the adult and responds emotionally to the story. The adult considers matters such as construction and char-acter development, but the "child" knows what it likes. The good picture book deals with universal feelings, just as adult literature does.

Many years ago, my assistant, Karen Shaw-Widman, came into my office at Viking with a manuscript. "I've been reading so much junk that this one really stood out. It has something. What do you think?" I read the manuscript as Karen watched.

By the third sentence ("Ronald Morgan, why are you crawling under the table like a snake?") I knew I was hearing a fresh voice. When I finished, I was smiling, and said to Karen: "You're right." We burst in on George Nicholson, the editorial director, and watched as he read *Today Was a Terrible Day*, grinning all the way. We were all excited, and when we'd calmed down a bit, we called the author, which is probably one of the best moments in an edi-tor's life—as well as the author's. We want to buy your manuscript! Patricia Reilly Giff was amazed and delighted, of course. (She later told me her mother had wanted to know how much we were going to charge her to publish the book. "They're paying *me*, Mom," she'd said.)

Later we found out that Giff had two novels ready to submit. After reading them, we bought *Fourth-Grade Celebrity* and *The Girl Who Knew It All*. Editors are looking for writers with promise, and we often find them in the picture book slush. It was clear that Giff was talented, but more important, her writing showed the spark that lifted her above the competition.

What was the "something" my assistant had admired in *Today*

Was a Terrible *Day?* The book, which dealt with a universal feel-ing—the inability of Ronald Morgan to do anything right one day in school—had humor and charm, was set in a real classroom, and had a satisfying ending for Ronald. The writing was simple and direct. It led poor Ronald through a day of disasters, such as eating the wrong lunch, flubbing on the baseball field, and even forgetting to water the teacher's plant. To make matters worse, he broke the plant when he finally did water it.

Does all this explain the "something" that won us over? Proba-bly not. The spark is an elusive quality. Maurice Sendak calls it a quickening that attracts and involves the reader, and makes him want to read the book over and over. All of us recognize the spark when we experience it. Perhaps it's as basic as life itself, which is, of course, far from simple. Giff's manuscript had life! It charmed us. It made us laugh as we recognized ourselves. And it showed us, subtly, that kindness toward another rewarded both giver and re-ceiver. The closest I can come to explaining the spark is that it springs from truth and satisfies our emotions.

Having been a teacher for over twenty years (and the mother of three), Giff understood children and knew classroom life inti-mately. Most important, she respected children and cared about them, and her concern is evident in all her books. They are without sentimentality, condescension, or a false idea of what children are like. Giff knows that children are people. Like the editor, she had a child inside herself, and remembered what it was like to be one.

You need not be a teacher or a parent to write effectively for children, but you have to be in touch with the child inside you so that you can experience the world in that special way again. It doesn't matter whether your hero is a child or an animal as long as the emotions are valid for the character. After checking *Books in Print* and seeing all the titles about mice, a writer once asked me whether this was a cue not to write another. "Rather than ask whether the world can use another mouse tale," I told her, "ask instead, 'Why mice?' "

The animals in children's stories often reflect types—the mouse is like a child in its powerlessness. This gives the young reader an immediate sense of identification with the plight of the animal (the same is true of rabbits, ducklings, and chicks). Keep this psycho-logical truth in mind if you want to write a story with animal char-acters. Editors frequently tell writers that their stories are anthropomorphic, which means giving human characteristics to animals or inanimate objects. What it really means is that your animal lacks psychological reality.

The editor and writer James Cross Giblin was once asked, "Is it okay if the animals in my story talk?" He answered: "It depends on what they have to say." Many animal tales are unsuccessful because writers fail to match the attributes of the animal character to its true or perceived nature, thinking it sufficient that the animal be cute and cuddly. Study the stories by Beatrix Potter, which are based on her own painstaking observations of small animals. Real rabbits eat vegetables in other people's gardens. Kittens are curious. Frogs catch bugs. Tune into any natural history program on TV, and you'll see that snakes eat frogs and mice and other helpless creatures: that's why they make good villains. So do foxes and wolves, though wolves, we know today, are not as bad as they were painted in the past, and probably would do better as heroes in a modern story. It's no accident that addlepated Henny-Penny is a chicken, Curious George is a monkey, and Charlotte is a spider. Their personalities fit the animals chosen to represent them. Keeping this in mind, make up your own list of animals and attributes. You'll soon see that you'll never lack a child audience for an animal tale, provided it has the spark.

Sometimes the spark comes from a new angle. Perhaps there's a story in an owl that's stupid or a tiger that's timid. Perhaps it's already been done. Animals in stories are substitutes for people, including children. Therefore you can have greater freedom, since the humor can be extended without hurting feelings, and storybook animals can behave in ways denied to children.

This is where your knowledge of what's gone before comes in and why you must visit the children's room at your library and read the books. You should also subscribe to a major children's reviewing medium such as *The Horn Book* or *Booklist*. You can't possibly keep up with all the new books, but you should try as best you can.

After animal stories, the most popular picture books for children are about children themselves. Find a way to observe children, either your own or others'. I once sat outside my local library and watched a group of kids play hide-and-seek on the lawn. Among the children were a pair of twin boys, Sean and Seamus. The names were changed, but they turned up in a book I was plotting for a packager. Betsy Byars once told me that the best material came from watching her children and their friends. "They say and do things I'd never think of in a million years."

Emily Arnold McCully has said, "Look at the world in your own way. Stay fresh, renew yourself, and don't get confused by trends."

Ask people to tell you stories of their childhood. Take notes or use a tape recorder. Don't trust your memory; sometimes nuances are lost or forgotten. Sit down and make a list of everything you can remember about your own childhood. William Kotzwinkle wrote a delightful book called *The Day the Gang Got Rich*, about a boy's finding five dollars. Don't we all love to find things? And what about losing them?

Ideas for stories about children are everywhere. Small-town newspapers are mines of material, and if you don't live in a small town, subscribe to a paper anyway; an out-of-state paper is best because you can be objective. Most writers keep a file full of clippings from small-town papers. Each story suggests a book idea, such as a boy getting his first haircut—from a woman barber. On the other hand, ideas are only germs of stories. It's what you do with them that counts. And never tell an editor that a newspaper article inspired you: we are looking for *fiction* and don't need to know your source.

If you can take an incident from life and develop it into a story, wonderful! But the best stories emerge not from incidents but from character. The lack of character development led to my downfall when I wrote about the pigeon that got its leg caught in a clam. The editor called the pigeon "passive." Passive characters are not interesting to read about and are best left to French novelists. In spite of the fact that it left home and went out to seek a more exciting life, my pigeon was passive. A yacht *happened* to be passing by, and it got a lift. It *happened* to get its leg caught in the clam. A passing sailor *happened* to rescue it, and offered it a chance to be his mascot. The pigeon *did nothing* to bring about the happiness it sought. It's what's wrong with the books some celebrities write: although the problems the children have are real, adults intervene to solve them in every case.

The cardinal rule of children's books for all ages is that the children have to solve their problems on their own. In real life, of course, parents take care of their children's needs. But it makes for boring storytelling! Can you imagine: "Billy wanted to go to the zoo. His mother took him. They had fun. The End." Instead: "Billy wanted to go to the zoo. But no one would take him." Why not? And what does Billy do? He should end up at the zoo because of something he's done. As an exercise in plotting, think of all the reasons Billy can't get to the zoo. (His mother is sick, the zoo is closed, etc.) Then how does Billy get around the obstacle? In solving this problem, Billy also solves another, secondary, problem. (The zookeeper lives next door, and he can't get to the zoo because his car is broken. Billy takes the zookeeper to the zoo on his tricycle.) This isn't much of a story, but I present it to show how Billy's plight can be made into a plot, and Billy can become an active hero.

Even Giff's manuscript about Ronald Morgan was guilty of having a passive hero. Ronald does a lot of dumb things, one after the other. In the original version, Giff had the teacher telling Ronald not to worry, that tomorrow would be better because it was her birthday. True to life, but dull. How were we going to fix the ending? When we were discussing a solution, Giff reminded me that Ronald was having trouble learning to read. In the published version, the teacher gives Ronald a note, and he reads it, which empowers him. The book ends with a final twist: Ronald decides to give the teacher a plant for her birthday. "I know she needs one," he says. Humor and the recognition on Ronald's part that he was responsible for his actions saved the book.

Another common problem with picture books is condescension. Don't write "the little girl" or "the little boy." Give your character a name. And don't use baby talk such as "his mommy" or "her daddy" or "tummy" or "itty-bitty." Children resent being talked down to as much as you do.

Condescension and passive heroes often go along with didacticism: teaching a lesson through a story. Books for children teach lessons all the time, but they must be taught subtly. A hundred years ago, children were given obvious moral lessons in their stories as a matter of course. Writers like Beatrix Potter and Lewis Carroll were among the earliest to rebel against this dreary tradition. Carroll made fun of the stuffy rules of behavior foisted on children, turning, for example, the Puritan poet Isaac Watt's "How doth the little bee improve each shining hour" into "How doth the little crocodile/Improve his shining tail." Potter's parents were typical Victorians, and it's a wonder that her stories are so unlike the norms of her time. Peter Rabbit's foray into Mr. MacGregor's garden passed muster among Victorian parents because Peter eventually gets punished—the modern reader also sees that Peter had a good time eating his fill in the garden. Alison Lurie put it in modern terms in her book *Don't Tell the Grown-Ups*:

> The great subversive works of children's literature suggest that there are other views of human life besides those of the shopping mall and the corporation. They mock current assumptions and express the imaginative, unconventional, noncommercial view of the world in its simplest and purest form. They appeal to the imaginative, questioning, rebellious child within all of us, renew our instinctive energy, and act as a force for change.

Other popular subjects for picture books are fairy- and folktales, songs, and narrative poems. You should know that in most cases when a "retold" tale is published, the artist has chosen it and retold it himself, or the editor has commissioned a writer to do it. Illustrators are always looking for stories to illustrate, and since they are usually not writers themselves, they fall back on public domain (no longer in copyright) material. It's rarely worth a writer's while to submit a retold familiar tale, like "Cinderella." On the other hand, an unusual tale may be just the thing an editor is looking for to give to an illustrator. Leo and Diane Dillon's artwork earned a Caldecott Medal in 1976 for the book *Why Mosquitoes Buzz in People's Ears*, based on the West African tale retold by Verna Aardema.

Nature is in the news, and there have been many books celebrating it, such as Robert McCloskey's *One Morning in Maine*. You may well have a lyrical manuscript about the rain or the sea that an editor will want to publish, but your chances of success with such a work are low if you are neither an illustrator nor a well-known writer. Given the high production costs of full-color picture books (around $50,000 for printing and binding), editors must look closely at the bottom line.

The same is true of stories written in verse. If you know anything about writing poetry, you know it requires talent and years of work to be good at it. Yet, because "it's just for children," verse manuscripts come pouring into publishers' offices. The narrative lines are usually less than distinguished, and the verses are not poetic but jingly, with easy rhymes and unnatural syntax such as "to him I said." T. S. Eliot, Theodore Roethke, and Richard Wilbur have all written verse narratives for children. *The Ox-cart Man*, illustrated by Barbara Cooney, won the Caldecott Medal, but Donald Hall's poem had appeared in the *New Yorker* first. With competition of this caliber, it's rare indeed for an editor to buy verse by an unknown writer.

Fiction is not the only way to reach young readers. Children have a great deal of curiosity and enjoy reading "information books," or nonfiction. If you have a desire to teach through books, consider writing nonfiction picture books. Susan Bonners, an artist and writer, won the American Book Award for her spectacular *A Penguin Year*, about the life cycle of penguins. Nonfiction picture books usually deal with history, biography, natural science, technology, and crafts. The writer presents these subjects in a simple way, usually focusing on one aspect rather than a panorama. Alice and Martin Provensen, a married author-illustrator team, won the Caldecott Medal for their magnificent illustrations in *The Glorious Flight*, the story of the first man to fly the English Channel.

Many writers, especially those unsure of their ability to write fiction, think a nonfiction picture book would be a snap to write. Not so. Like Bonners and the Provensens, you must choose a subject that will appeal to small children, your writing must be lively and terse, and you must find a subject that hasn't been done a zillion times. Do all this in a few thousand words, because librarians and teachers—and parents—are definitely looking for intelligent nonfiction for readers between the ages of five and eight.

A slavish concern for "rules" leads many writers to be unduly concerned about word counts and page counts for the various forms they are writing in, and to them I say only that picture books can run from zero words (wordless) up to a few thousand words. On average, they're only a few pages long.

One writer asked me, "Why are publishers always talking about thirty-two pages?" Because books are made up of "signatures," which has nothing to do with autographs. A signature is a group of pages (never less than four) printed at one time and folded into a unit that is then bound into a book. Most picture books are made up of one 32-page signature. The text and art are printed on two sides of a big piece of paper; each side holds 16 pages. When folded and trimmed according to the "imposition," or sequence, of the artwork, the result is a total of 32 pages. To keep costs and prices down, publishers prefer to adhere to one signature. Picture books can run 40, 48, or 64 pages, but the ideal for the publisher is 32. Of these, two to six pages are taken up by the title page, copyright, and so on (the front matter), leaving about 26 pages (or 13 double-page spreads) for text and illustrations.

With this in mind, it's a good idea (and fun) for the writer to make a dummy of her manuscript. Fold eight pieces of paper in half, and you'll have a 32-page blank dummy. Then cut up a copy of your manuscript and lay out the text on the 13 spreads. See how your story flows and whether there's enough change of action for an illustrator to work with. A common flaw in picture book manuscripts is the long stretches of dialog, narrative, or description where little happens. Remember that the artist will show how people are dressed and what the setting looks like.

Imagine that you are the illustrator. How would you illustrate, for example, a long stretch of text about a child thinking? Or two people talking? Or an interminable description? Once you see how the text fits the book, you'll be able to rewrite and cut back on long passages. If your text has too many words, be ruthless and weed out the unnecessary ones. On the other hand, you may find you're off to a good start with your story, but that it sags in the middle—nothing happens for an illustrator to work with. It's time to rethink the story.

When you retype the manuscript, you might want to quadru-ple-space between the pages you envision; showing the page breaks in this way helps the editor to visualize how the book will work out with illustrations.

Again, do not include detailed instructions for the illustrator. The story has to be complete as you have told it, because it might be read on an audiocassette or on the radio, where the art is not visible. Because of this, you should read the story aloud to yourself to hear how it sounds. When you are satisfied, send the publisher the manuscript, typed in the standard way, on white bond. Do not send your dummy, unless you are an illustrator.

Many a beginning writer thinks that if her manuscript were sent in with illustrations by a friend, it would stand a better chance. Nothing is farther from the truth, but writers have difficulty accepting this. Ask yourself this: Suppose the editor thinks the story is wonderful, but that the art is not? (Or vice versa.) A while ago, an agent sent me an illustrated manuscript. The art was superb, but the text was terrible. When I told her I was interested in the artist, the agent told me that other editors had responded as I had, and because of this, the writer and artist were no longer friends.

Editors buy stories; editors buy art. The royalty is divided between the author and the illustrator. But rarely do we buy a picture book as a package, except from established teams. Most children's publishing houses have art directors whose specialty is keeping up with illustrators. The editor and art director will discuss possibilities and will choose the best artist for the story. For marketing reasons, we might want to use a famous artist to compensate for the unknown name of the writer. It is unrealistic to expect a publisher to expend a huge amount of money on a book when neither the artist nor the writer is known. Someday, when you and your illustrator friend are launched on your careers, you may be able to collaborate, but for now, please don't do it.

This chapter has been full of negative advice, but I offer it so that you may save yourself a great deal of frustration. You *can* lift your picture book above the hundreds in the slush pile. Work on your story, tone, and theme. Avoid the pitfalls of anthropomorphism, condescension, didacticism, and sentimentality. Have fun with your characters—sometimes they'll surprise you. Then read your story aloud and see where your tongue has trouble with the words and sentences. Be ruthless and eliminate each unnecessary word. Write and rewrite.

Editors are always looking for good picture book manuscripts, which are as rare in the slush pile as pearls in oysters. But when we find one, we leap for joy, because a good book for children is worth more than its weight in pearls.

4 The Reading Is Easy

NOT SO LONG ago, books that readers aged six to nine wanted to read on their own were scarce on bookstore and library shelves. While the six-year-olds still found picture books delightful, and some were turning the pages of "beginning readers," older children began to yearn for books that looked more grown-up.

"Amy's almost in third grade," a friend told me. "She wants to read real books, with chapters and not so many pictures. What can you recommend?" There wasn't much for Amy fifteen years ago, though I did recommend *Pippi Longstocking* by Astrid Lindgren and Joan Aiken's Arabel books.

By the mid-eighties this scarcity was ending. Patricia Reilly Giff, who was then teaching reading to second graders, told me she didn't have enough interesting trade books to offer her students, many of whom were poor readers, except for the Nate the Great books by Marjorie Sharmat, the Dorrie and the Blue Witch series by Patricia Coombs, the popular chapter books by Clyde Robert Bulla, and a handful of others. "I guess you'll have to write them," I told her. Giff had already published two hardcover novels for fourth graders at Delacorte and picture books at Viking and Dutton. When Beverly Horowitz, who was then at Dell, suggested Giff follow a group of children through a typical school year, month by month, she dived into writing her Kids of the Polk Street School paperback series. Published at the rate of one a month, the Polk Street School books comprised ten titles, running from September to June. They filled a need, they were funny, and kids loved them. Reviewers and teachers were enthusiastic, too, and the books were later published in hardcover, all at once. Sales are in the millions, and Giff went on to extend the series. She also wrote several series using other characters from the original ten books all illustrated with Blanche Sims's lively drawings.

Many publishers suddenly realized that a virtually untapped market lay waiting for them. True, some already had long-standing beginning reader series like I Can Read from Harper's. Also available for six- to nine-year-old readers, of course, were many fine picture books with sophisticated, long texts and glorious full-color illustrations on every page, which often spilled over onto double-page spreads. These difficult texts were meant to be read aloud, because small children could not read them on their own.

For example, the 1973 Caldecott Award Book *Duffy and the Devil*, by Harve and Margot Zemach, has the following sentence:

> The door of a cottage flew open and out ran a blubbering, bawling girl chased by an old woman who was clouting her with a broom and shouting, "You lazy bufflehead, you!"

Duffy and the Devil is a forty-page book adapted from a Cornish folktale. A good reader in the second or third grade could certainly master it with some help from an adult. But its mouth-filling humorous words ("gashly," "confloption," and "gallivants") demand that it be read aloud. We can imagine children grinning at the sounds. A book like this is what teachers and librarians call a stretch book: it introduces children to a different culture and expands their vocabulary and knowledge. The publisher calls it a picture book because of the quantity and quality of the art—four-color pen-and-wash illustrations—and the size—$8\frac{1}{2} \times 10\frac{5}{8}$. But many seven- and eight-year-olds call it a baby book and won't pick it up.

On the other hand, Wanda Gag's *Millions of Cats* is an example of a picture book that a first or second grader can read by herself. The vocabulary is simple, the art is in black and white, and because it is smaller, it doesn't look so babyish. The book is about an old man and woman who decide they want a cat for company. One of my students expressed shock at the amount of violence in the story: millions of cats fight one another to the death as they compete for the place of honor in the couple's home. But the important thing about the book is the love between the old people, which they wind up sharing with a scrawny cat that didn't join the fray. According to *The Arbuthnot Anthology of Children's Literature*, *Millions of Cats*, published in 1928, "paved the way for the 'golden years' of the thirties when picture books achieved a new importance." Given that the "golden years" were also the years of the Great Depression and World War II, the violence in the book was a prescient mirror of what was to come, and children sensed that love was the only antidote.

Once a child is off the lap, she needs books she can read on her own. She wants to feel grown-up, able to read books that look like those in the hands of older children. Paperbacks fit the bill perfectly, of course. Children of six to nine still enjoy looking at illustrations, and for them an illustrated storybook or a "chapter book" is just right. An illustrated storybook is not a picture book. In a picture book the art is integral; the child can almost "read" the book simply by looking at the pictures. In a storybook, like *Joey's Head* by Gladys Cretan, the story outweighs the art.

Many writers are confused about the differences between writing stories for picture books, storybooks, and "chapter books." Today's picture book is likely to have a very short text, and one hardly hears the term "storybook" any longer, although they are still being published. It's important to understand that an editor can choose how to publish a particular story based on considerations of cost and today's market.

For example, an editor may decide to publish a story like "Hansel and Gretel" (the version in the *Blue Fairy Book* by Andrew Lang runs about three thousand words) with a condensed text of a thousand or so words and glorious full-color double-page spreads on eight-by-ten-inch pages by a famous illustrator as a thirty-two–page *picture book*. Or she might choose to publish it with fewer illustrations on a seven-by-nine-inch page and the complete Lang text as a thirty-two–page *storybook*. In the latter case, there would be few or no glorious double spreads in full color; instead there might be spot drawings, in color or black and white, sprinkled throughout the book, which would cost less to produce. Or, responding to the demand for chapter books, an editor might decide to make the story easier to read by rewriting it with a simpler vocabulary and shorter sentences and breaking it into brief chapters. In this case the story might be set in large type on five-by-eight-inch pages with folios (numbers) to make the story look more like a "real" book, run forty-eight pages, have a limited amount of artwork, and be called a *chapter book*. Today's editor is likely to either edit a long story down to picture book size, or make it a chapter book. Therefore, the writer should concentrate on brief texts for picture books or longer ones that can stand as chapter books.

In my view, the true chapter book is a short novel, which can run from forty-eight to over a hundred book pages, with perhaps a dozen pages devoted to black-and-white art; the manuscripts run from forty to eighty pages or more. These "real" books, or short novels, are for children to read on their own, and the writing is simple—which is not the same as easy. Stephanie Spinner, who is executive editor at Random House and associate publisher of Knopf books for young readers, told me that she was looking for clarity, simplicity, and a good story with lots of action for the Stepping Stone books. "In my imagination the text is like an iceberg with only a fraction above the surface and the rest—all the work that goes into simplifying the text and making it readable—below the surface."

As I worked with Giff on the Polk Street books, she taught me that children who are learning to read like lots of white space, large type, and short words and sentences. Repetition of words helps, and the length of words is important. Giff, because of her experience teaching reading, is able to calculate the reading levels of her books and will often weigh the use of one word over another. Her books do not read like textbooks, however, because she has devised her own way of storytelling, using natural speech rhythms and even sentence fragments or one-word sentences. In this passage from *The Beast in Ms. Rooney's Room*, Richard "Beast" Best is being taunted by his sister, Holly, and her friend, Joanne.

> "Polk Street," Richard said. "That's a president's name?" He shook his head. "He's got a funny first name."
>
> Holly started to laugh. She leaned against Joanne. "I told you, Joanne," she said after a minute. "He's a dummy."
>
> "Not Polk Street," Joanne said. "The school is *on* Polk Street. They're both named for President Polk. President James K. Polk."
>
> "Don't try to tell him," Holly said. "He doesn't even know George Washington."
>
> "I do so," Richard said.
>
> "Or Christopher Columbus."
>
> "I do so."

"Who was he?"
Richard stopped. "A president."

Readability is important if you want to sell the greatest number of books. Many more fifth graders are reading at the second-grade level than second graders at the fifth-grade level. If you have a word processor, you can buy a program that will calculate reading levels for you. Or you could send your manuscript to a readability laboratory like Swinburn in Charlottesville, Virginia. Or you could get your hands on the Dale-Chall and Spache word lists, which contain words like "bobolink" but not words like "pizza." Or learn the Frye readability formula, which uses sentence length and syllable counts to come up with a score. But such precision isn't necessary for trade book purposes, and may even make your writing as bland as the textbooks for which the formulas were originally devised.

The best way to achieve a given reading level is to study published books at the level you wish to reach. Many publishers indicate the reading levels of their books on the covers, jackets, or copyright pages; look for the letters RL and a number—2.4 means a book is capable of being read by a second-grade student in the fourth month of school.

As a first step compare the passage from *The Beast in Ms. Rooney's Room* with the one-sentence passage from *Duffy and the Devil*. You can see at a glance that with its thirty-two words and forty-three syllables the sentence from *Duffy* is at an extremely high reading level. (You'll also see, however, that most of the words are of one syllable, and three of the longest begin with B: "blubbering," "bawling," and "bufflehead," which makes them memorable once the child has learned them.)

So don't forget to use common sense. You cannot judge a reading level on the basis of one sentence or one passage that may be atypical. Some other factors that govern readability are the size of the typeface, the number of words on a page, the presence of art that depicts the words, the complexity of the material, and the familiarity of certain multisyllabic words. For example, most children already know the meaning of "yesterday," so it may be easier for them to read and understand than a smaller word like "iron." Context is important, too. If you use a word like "iron," you should provide clues to indicate that you are talking about a metal. Varying sentence lengths is a good idea, too. Note that in the passage from *Beast* an occasional long sentence is bracketed by short ones.

Writing a good book for the beginning reader depends on more than just achieving the proper reading level. After all, many of Hemingway's works are on a second-grade reading level, and Plato's on a fourth-grade reading level. You must also be aware of a child's interest level.

Again, do your market research. Pore over publishers' catalogs and find out which publishers are actively seeking what kind of material for ages six to nine. Nonfiction for this age group is enjoying a revival, and that may be right for you. Or you might want to try a long story, a collection of short tales, or a short novel. Different children in the same grade read with varying degrees of proficiency: we have the gifted reader, the average reader, and the slow reader—not to mention the nonreader. At the moment, the emphasis seems to be on providing books for average or slow readers. Five years from now, editors may be looking for books with richer vocabularies and more complex sentences for gifted readers. In truth, they are always looking for both kinds of books, and it's you, the writer, who should decide on what you like to write. Here are some points to keep in mind.

Interest level: Children of this age are absorbed in the world immediately around them, which is why stories about family life and school, like the Polk Street School books, are so popular. At the same time, their horizons are expanding to some degree. Below are some popular categories or genres for young readers in grades two, three, and maybe four.

Animal stories: Not too long ago, a sales rep for Dell came into the office with bad news. "I can't move those Olga da Polga [Michael Bond] books for anything," he said. The reason: children of six to nine who were capable of reading the text considered themselves too old for stories with animal characters—in this case, guinea pigs. Today's children tend to think animal stories are babyish, especially when the animals are soft and cuddly. They don't seem to mind amphibians like those in Arnold Lobel's Frog and Toad books and Jane Yolen's Commander Toad series or Ninja turtles, dinosaurs, sharks, and other animals whose habitat is TV or the movies. You may protest at this generalization: of course there are still children aged six to nine who enjoy *Winnie the Pooh*. But not as many as there used to be, thanks, no doubt, to the mass media. A traditional publisher enjoys nothing more than a good animal story like *The Wind in the Willows*, but experience has shown that sales will be low in mass market, although librarians, who also love animal stories, will buy them. My advice is to think twice if you want to write an easy-reading book with furry animals as the main characters.

Fantasy: At what age is it more appropriate to have fantasies than in early childhood? Whether folktale or Greek myth, these stories have the power to engage children on a deep, symbolic level. Excellent collections of fairy tales already exist, though most are not at the easy-reading level. But beware: many of these tales are not yet appropriate for second graders because of their complexity. And as I mentioned earlier, familiar tales are usually the domain of the illustrator. Given the popularity of the strange creatures in movies like *E. T.*, a writer can try to provide stories with strong fantasy elements on a higher level than what is found in the mass media. Little fantasy has been done in the easy-reader category so far, and you may be breaking new ground. On the other hand, not all editors are fond of fantasy, so research the market thoroughly and be sure you understand the rules for writing fantasy.

Historical fiction: As they begin to learn that there's a wider world outside their ken, children develop an interest in the past. People like George Washington and Abraham Lincoln take on mythic stature, and young children are interested in learning more about them. Stories and novels set in historical times can find an audience provided the information is accurate and the story exciting, as in Nathaniel Benchley's *Sam the Minuteman*, which was first published by Harper as an I Can Read in 1969. There is still a need for historical fiction set in North America that features females, minorities, and especially Native Americans, to redress the balance of years of publishing books about white men and boys taking part in historical events.

Horror: Unfortunately, horror stories are often grouped with science fiction and fantasy, but they are usually an inferior subgroup, sometimes called Sci-Fi, a pejorative term for science fiction. (*Godzilla* is sci-fi, for example.) Obviously, graphic horror of the Stephen King variety is not suitable for small children, but they have long enjoyed spooky stories, such as "The Teeny Tiny Woman," an old English ghost tale. A good monster story can be cathartic for some children who, after all, often have frightening nightmares; but they should not scare children to death. Halloween stories are always popular, and horror combined with humor can be a lot of fun as in Stephen Mooser's paperback series, the Creepy Creature Club, which is less about horror than about a group of children who are so fascinated by monsters that they form a club.

Humor: This is the natural way to go for this age group. Kids of this age love slapstick and humor that is broad. Robert Newton Peck's Soup books cater to this taste at the upper end of the age group. Betsy Byars's *The Golly Sisters* is an energetic tale of two sisters who go to the Old West to entertain and bring along their sibling rivalries. Tall tales are just right for these readers. They love the exaggeration found in the beloved old storybooks like *The Loudest Noise in the World*, *The 500 Hats of Bartholomew Cubbins*, and *Millions of Cats*.

Mystery: Elizabeth Levy's Something Queer series and David Adler's Cam Jensen easy-reading mysteries kicked off the genre for contemporary young readers, and Peggy Parrish's books, though harder to read, have long been popular. Even the Bobbsey Twins are back in new packaging. As you may be aware, mysteries now proliferate, and are therefore harder to place. Unless you have something unique to offer, beware of Publisher's Glut in this category. However, I suspect there's always room for another one, so if you want to attempt this, remember that mysteries for this age should concentrate on simple "crimes," such as a missing pet. Neither the child nor anyone else should ever be faced with real danger or violence. We are still in an age of innocents here. Keep it light.

Nonfiction: Since this is an age that loves to learn, nonfiction is welcome at most houses. Science, biography, and history seem to be the most popular subjects for this age group, and bountiful illustrations are necessary.

Problem novels: Although, unfortunately, children need books about some of the current societal problems, like child abuse, they find it hard to deal with such problems except as it might affect them personally. Unemployment is an abstraction until, as in *Tight Times* by Barbara Shook Hazen and *Ramona and Her Father* by Beverly Cleary, it hits close to home. Being human, children want to solve problems, but some are too difficult and encouraging children to take on more responsibility than they are able to handle can lead to frustration and feelings of powerlessness. *50 Simple Things Kids Can Do To Save the Earth*, for example, sometimes places too much of a burden on children to clean up after their elders.

Sports: From earliest childhood, readers are also young athletes, no matter how developed their abilities may be. Watch toddlers as they run, jump, and climb. Physical education begins in some schools in kindergarten, with simple Mickey Mouse aerobics, progressing to team sports. Outside of school, some children are involved in Little League, Pee Wee Hockey, and Pop Warner football; whether they play or not, most children are aware of professional athletics and, of course, the Olympic Games. Publishers have begun to publish books with sports themes for the very youngest, and this is an area you might wish to explore. Sports can teach values as well as athletic skill, and are an excellent vehicle through which to reach early readers. Sports not only promote fitness—so important in this TV-bound era—but give children a sense of self-esteem. Don't forget that disabled children can also take part in games. Try not to overemphasize athletic prowess and competition in your writing. It's important to convey to children that how you play the game means more than winning and that sportsmanship is an ideal to strive for.

Whatever subject you pick, write the best story you can with well-developed characters and lots of action. The same rules for writing apply to books for early readers as do those for any other work. As Frances Hanna, a Canadian literary agent, told me, "A children's book must have a magic of its own. It's moving, memorable, and almost always visual—a vivid and original image of something physical that brings back a memory. It also captures a moment that is so moving it can bring you to tears because you empathize with the character."

Study the successful books, and then sit down and write. And be sure to have as much fun writing them as you hope they will be to read.

5 Characters,
Conflict, and Structure

BEGINNING AROUND THE age of nine, children seem to open their eyes and look at the larger world around them. This reflects their ability to get around on their own. No longer do they have to ask adults for permission to cross the street: they can get on their bicycles and ride off to visit friends, special places, or anywhere their fancies take them. When they are at home they can do the same through books, Emily Dickinson's "frigate" to "lands away." There's no limit on children's imaginations, and no limit on yours. What are they going to read?

The best book begins with characters, characters who want something. They spend the rest of the book trying to get it, while other people or events conspire to keep them from getting what they want.

Over and over again, you will hear from editors, "Know your characters." Once I pointed out to an author that a scene where a minor character, a policeman, interrogated a girl was unconvincing in her novel. The writer went home and later said, "I spent hours writing everything I knew about that cop: what he ate for breakfast, where he went to school, whom he married. None of it showed up in the book, but I knew who he was when I rewrote that scene." This time around, the scene worked.

In her 1893 essay "On Writing Fiction for Children," reprinted in the July 1988 issue of *The Writer*, Maria Molesworth, author of *The Cuckoo Clock* and other books, said,

> I generally begin by finding names for all my personages. I marshal them before me and call the roll, to which each an-

swers in turn, and then I feel I have my "troupe" complete, and I proceed to take them more in detail. I live with them as much as I can, often for weeks, before I have done more than write down their names. I listen to what they talk about to each other and in their own homes, not with the intention of writing it down, but by way of getting to know them well.

More recently, in *Death in the Afternoon* (1932), Ernest Hemingway warned: "A writer should create living people; people, not characters. A *character* is a caricature. If a writer can make people live, there may be no great characters in his book, but it is possible that his book will remain as a whole; as an entity; as a novel."

The average age for a protagonist in a middle-grade novel is twelve. This is purely for marketing reasons: children like to read about people who are their age or slightly older; rarely will they enjoy reading about younger characters. An exception is Beverly Cleary's *Ramona the Pest*, about a kindergartner; readers of this book are usually in the third grade. They say they enjoy reading about what it was like "back then." On the other hand, Nancy Drew is sixteen, and the books about her are especially popular with fifth graders, who can't wait to be sixteen, too. Twelve is also the age of the reader for whom a publisher decides whether to market a book as one for readers of nine to thirteen or as a young adult book, for readers twelve and up. Sometimes the same book can fit into either category. Don't worry about this. The publisher will position the book where it will sell the most copies. But here's a tip: if your protagonist is under twelve, try to avoid mentioning her age; let the reader project her own age onto the character.

All the categories summarized at the end of the previous chapter are valid for middle-grade readers, but the subjects should be treated in greater depth. Age levels also denote interest levels, and have nothing to do with reading levels. Many adults can read only at the second-grade level, and some children can read at the high-school level. *Age levels deal primarily with the subject matter*, not with the readability of a book. Age levels also reflect the mental and physical growth of a reader, and often (not always) are approximately the same as the age of the protagonist.

In his *Writing Books for Young People*, James Cross Giblin points out that nonfiction for young adults fell by the wayside when library funding was cut in the 1970s, but that nonfiction for younger readers is popular. The books must have "visual appeal," he says; that is, they must be heavily illustrated, to appeal to today's young reader. And Melanie Kroupa, of Joy Street Books, has said that she wants "nonfiction that makes a reader sit up and take notice." For a finished book running from 64 to 96 pages, many of them with illustrations, a manuscript should be about 25 to 65 pages long, which doesn't leave the writer much room for exploring large issues.

In addition, a nonfiction book usually has "back matter," such as charts, bibliographies, and an index. The writer is responsible for providing photographs and the back matter, with the exception of the index. Publishers usually prefer to use professional indexers, and will deduct the cost from your royalties.

Picture research is an important part of the nonfiction writer's job. You can find free or inexpensive photographs or historical illustrations at the Library of Congress, state, county, and municipal historical societies, museums, and local newspapers. However, illustrations are often copyrighted, and you must obtain permission to use them, pay the fees, and credit the copyright owners in your book.

Sometimes a writer believes a book is called for because an important anniversary is looming ahead. If you have such an idea you should probably begin working on it five to eight *years* before the anniversary. In the spring of 1990, I began to receive proposals for books about Columbus's 1492 voyage. It was much too late then. Back in 1984 Congress had already passed a bill (HR 1492) establishing a Christopher Columbus Quincentenary Jubilee Commission; the lawmakers knew it would take time to prepare for the big day. For a book to reach its market, primarily schools and libraries, it must be *in production* about three years before the date. Since it will take you several years to do the research, write the book, and sell it to a publisher, you must begin early. It then takes over a year to edit and produce the book and eighteen months after the book is published for it to be reviewed, ordered, and shipped to libraries. Therefore a book about Columbus should have been published in 1990 or 1991. This would allow a year or so of hardcover sales before paperback publication in 1992.

It is rarely worth writing a book solely to commemorate an anniversary. Libraries already own books on the subject to be commemorated; will they need another one? For example, 1995 is the

fiftieth anniversary year of the end of World War II and the drop-
ping of the atomic bombs on Hiroshima and Nagasaki. The mass
media (TV, magazines, newspapers) have planned special coverage
of these events. But will children's books on these topics sell out-
standingly well as a result? Sometimes they do, if the event is re-
lated to classroom studies. Other times, the effect on sales is negligible. Will anyone want to read your book about the atomic bomb
in 1996? Only if it's a good book.

Editors are relaxed about "special events," because many of us
already have books on our backlists that we can promote in the
special year. We do not actively seek "anniversary" books. But if a
good one comes along, with enough time to spare, we may well be
interested.

In her *New York Times Book Review* article about children's books
on the American Revolution and the Constitution in 1987 (the anniversary year of the Constitutional Convention), Pauline Maier,
professor of history at M.I.T., wrote:

> Surely history should be well written. Joy in language knows
> no age, and the most successful children's books—whose lines
> stay in the mind when childhood is long gone—have always
> been skillfully composed. History books should be appropri-
> ate to their readers' ages, and they should be accurate. That
> is, they should get the basic facts right and provide an under-
> standing of events that accords with known evidence.

Be prepared, then, to research your book thoroughly. Reviewers, teachers, librarians, and even your child readers will pounce
on any error of fact.

Perhaps the best way to teach children is through historical fiction. Pick an event that excites you, do your research, and create a
young protagonist to witness it. For example, when I found out that
Columbus's thirteen-year-old son Fernando had actually traveled
with him on the fourth and final voyage and had written a book
about his father, Fernando became the hero of my book *The High
Voyage*.

Writers of historical fiction have an unusual problem when they
try to re-create the past. People through the ages have much in
common, but a fifteenth-century Spanish boy will not have the
same attitudes as a twentieth-century American woman. Although
Fernando was humane enough to appreciate Native Americans as

people, he still considered them savages who should defer to Europeans and be converted to Christianity. Columbus's wholesale baptizing of the "Indians" he encountered—whether or not they understood what was happening—is not behavior we would sanction today. How is the writer to handle these situations if she wants to be true to the time she writes about? Sometimes the only way out is to append a note of explanation at the back of the book.

James Lincoln Collier and Christopher Collier ran into a similar problem when they wrote the Arabus trilogy about a black family before, during, and after the American Revolution. Not to use the word "nigger" would have been false to the spirit of the time, yet we all found it distasteful. They explained this in afterwords to the books, under the title "How Much of This Book Is True?"

Good historical fiction re-creates a time through detail, characterization, and the subtle use of language. We assume our forebears were intelligent people, and we portray them with respect. According to the Colliers, since there are no aural records of the past, we cannot know how they spoke, although we do know how they wrote. The use of dialect or archaic language sets them apart from us, so the good writer depends on sinewy contemporary prose. Although all of us speak in one dialect or another, depending on where we live, we all read standard English, and that is the language the writer should use. However, standard English does not mean the language you hear on TV. Columbus or Thomas Jefferson would never say "traveling turns me on" or "Man, that's gross." For example, the use of "presently" to mean "now" is fairly recent. If Benjamin Franklin used it, he would mean "in the near future," nor would he say "disinterested" when he meant "uninterested."

In addition to watching out for anachronistic language, the writer must also worry about anachronistic details. Columbus sailed by the stars. He had no clock. His compass was a lodestone. Most of the food his sailors ate was European: no corn on the cob, no beans, no tomatoes, not even potatoes, because Europeans hadn't discovered them yet. Research is not just a matter of looking up names and dates: you must know how people looked, what they wore, and even how they smelled (there were no deodorants in either Columbus's or Washington's time; on the other hand, people in the past probably didn't notice body odor as much as we do today).

Unfortunately, historical fiction is not a particularly popular genre among young people, though they will read it as part of their school assignments. Hardcover publishers believe it should be published because it is a valuable part of our literary tradition. Paperback publishers are usually reluctant to buy reprint rights because, unless the author is well known, it will sell poorly in softcover editions, especially in the chains, where the kids are buying the books. Still, a market exists, and if you love history, it may be the genre for you.

In writing any kind of fiction, keep in mind that your protagonist need not be likable, but she should be someone the reader can identify with and be sympathetic to, as in the case of sulky Mary in *The Secret Garden*, surely one of the most beloved books of all time. No doubt Frances Hodgson Burnett purposely made Mary disagreeable because she understood that unhappy children often were unpleasant, and who among us has never been unhappy? When Mary meets sickly Colin, our sympathies go out to her, because he's even sulkier than she is. But as the book goes on, the secret garden works its charm, and we find the characters growing more likable as they overcome their disabilities. Their maturation mirrors that of all the young readers who have adored this book, in spite of its many flaws and long paragraphs. *The Secret Garden* illustrates an essential point about children's books: *characters must grow and change*. This is as true today as it was when *The Secret Garden* was written.

Give your hero a conflict: it is the essence of memorable fiction. The classic conflicts are of four types: man against man, man against nature, man against society, and man against himself. Often I've read a manuscript and, in spite of its many good qualities, felt something—a tension—was missing. The problem most often was the lack of a well-defined conflict.

In *Are You There, God? It's Me, Margaret*, Judy Blume gave her protagonist several problems, including her desire to get her period and a conflict over choosing a religion. The first happens to her— she has no control over her body—but her decision about the second is the result of much inner struggle (girl against herself). In like manner, Hansel and Gretel, abandoned in the woods, must find their way to safety (children against nature; children against adults). Huckleberry Finn must make a momentous decision about whether to betray his slave friend, Jim (boy against himself; boy against society). It is on such conflicts that memorable books turn, and if there is one thing that distinguishes all good contemporary books for young people, it is that the hero must solve the problem on his own.

When my friends and I were ten and read *Elsie Dinsmore*, we had long conversations about Elsie's refusal to play the piano for her beloved father because it was Sunday and she believed in honoring the Sabbath. Even though we personally thought Elsie was old-fashioned, we identified with her internal struggle. When she fainted on the piano bench, we cheered her bravery in defying her father to satisfy her conscience. More recently, in *Courage, Dana*, Susan Beth Pfeffer has her hero agonize over whether to tell on her classmate, whom she has seen writing graffiti on school property.

Little children may be reassured when the woodcutter rushes in to save Little Red Riding Hood and her grandmother. But a contemporary retelling of the tale would show not a *deus ex machina* like the woodcutter, but the girl saving her grandmother. Our girls today must be Gretels, our boys Hucks. In *The Disappearance of Childhood*, Neil Postman writes that children ape the outward appearance of adulthood because they are surrounded by a society that emphasizes the superficial aspects of maturity, such as clothing. True maturity is inner growth, and good books for children show this. Adults can be supportive in books as the Cheshire Cat was in *Alice*, but they must not interfere with the child's resolution of the conflict.

Betsy Byars has said,

> I came to realize that to make the story more dramatic I had to put the character on his own. Thus began an exodus of parents possibly unequaled in children's literature. Parents went to Hunter City to give birth, to Europe on holidays, to Ohio to work, to Detroit to seek work. I favored occupations involving travel, like truck driving and country-western singing, and fell back on pneumonia, plane crashes, car accidents, divorce, and coal mine disasters.

Joan Aiken is even more ruthless. She makes her children orphans whenever she can. No matter how you get rid of parents, remember that you're doing so because children can't always count on adults. And no matter how good a parent you might be, your children have problems they don't want *you* to solve, because part of achieving maturity is developing good judgment and self-reliance. Children know this, if only subconsciously.

Pippi Longstocking, who is only half-orphaned, tries to instill independent thinking and self-confidence in her sheltered middle-class friends, Tommy and Annika. The fact that Pippi's judgment is often wrong is part of the teaching, because readers are shocked at what she does and are forced to think about what is right or wrong. Children know that Pippi Longstocking is a fantasy, with a big "what if?" Her mother is dead and her father is a sea captain. She lives on her own with a monkey and a horse and has superhuman strength and a chest full of gold. It's clear that Pippi can make her own rules. Real children know they can't, but delight in imagining what it would be like if they could.

Pippi is not real; nothing ever gets her down. Nor does she grow and change. If you are writing about a real child, she must have good points and weak points. It is this blend that results in complex characters worth reading about, characters who are as alive as people.

"When an author's voice seems genuine, without self-consciousness," says Bebe Willoughby, an editor and writer, "I pay immediate attention to the manuscript. I also want to be moved enough so that I can't put the manuscript down. Should this occur, I usually buy a manuscript even if it needs a lot of work." Luckily, many editors enjoy helping writers strengthen the structure or character development or conflict of a manuscript with potential. Sometimes the flaw may be caused by an oversight, as in a recent submission in which a boy is devastated because his mother is terminally ill and in the hospital. The writer "forgot" the mother: she doesn't appear in a single scene, either as a memory or in actuality. Instead, the writer concentrates on how the boy handled his life without her. But if we don't know how the boy felt about his mother as shown through interaction with her, can we care what happens?

In contrast, in Zilpha Keatley Snyder's *And Condors Danced*, Carly, the hero, feels guilty when her mother dies because she doesn't love her, and never has. Her mother did not love her, and abandoned Carly to the care of a beloved aunt. Snyder has the courage to be unsentimental about maternal and filial love.

Wendy Lamb, an editor and writer, has said, "A book is necessarily false," echoing Plato's assertion that poets are liars. The events didn't happen (or if they did, not in that exact way), and the people never existed. Yet the best books, like Snyder's, are true on another level: it is how people behave, it is how people feel. "The challenge is to make the voice sound real, yet not inarticulate," Lamb went on to say, "because in speech, people, especially children, are often rambling, vague, and repetitive."

The writer must also understand a child's sense of priorities. The same event is viewed differently by adults and children.

Before setting a character into motion, the writer should consider the choice of point of view, based on who is observing the action. It is usually advisable to keep to one point of view in a book for children because this results in a tighter, more suspenseful book. When everything is seen through the eyes of one character, readers are caught up in his emotions, which makes him come alive.

Compare, for example, these lines, where Jennifer Scrimshaw is the protagonist:

> Her mother sneezed. Jennifer looked up. Was her mother catching a cold?

> Her mother sneezed. Jennifer looked up. Am I catching a cold? Mrs. Scrimshaw wondered.

By switching from Jennifer's point of view to that of her mother's in the second example, the writer has broken the link between the reader and the hero. You must keep the reader's attention focused on your character.

Maintaining one point of view is easy in a first-person novel, but it is difficult to establish a strong sense of character, since the narrator is usually talking about the other people in the book. In some first-person novels, of which *Rebecca* by Daphne du Maurier is a prime example, the narrator doesn't even have a name. Also, in a novel where the hero is in danger, there's a loss of suspense, since obviously the narrator has survived to tell the story. Then, too, the writer is limited to "knowing" only that which the hero can observe or be told, which restricts literary freedom. Still, first-person is popular with older children and teenagers because the direct voice is an invitation to intimacy. There's no rule against using the first person in books for younger children, but if the main character is too young, his vocabulary and experience will be limited, as will the writer be if he tries to write in his voice. One way around this problem is to have an older sibling or friend tell the story about a small child.

Multiple viewpoints or that of an omniscient narrator are sometimes used by children's writers. Betsy Byars frequently has three
points of view in her novels and handles the switches in viewpoint
superbly. But too often writers fail, because in such short books
multiple viewpoints can weaken the structure of the story, while
one character can carry it all.

Before you begin writing, consider the matter of point of view
and try out different ones to see which feels the best. Take a hard
look at your multiple-viewpoint manuscript. If you confined all the
observations to only one character, would the manuscript be tighter
and more dramatic? In my experience, this is usually the case.
Drafts can be burned once they've served their purpose, and no one
need ever see your false starts as you set your characters in motion.
One writer told me that he writes each page of his books at least
seven times. "I may realize, when I get to page thirty-five," he said,
"that I've got to develop a new idea. I simply go back to page one
and begin writing all over again to plant it. This happens several
times in the same book, but usually by the seventh round, I'm sure
where I'm going."

In addition to your hero, you will have other characters, who
may be older or younger than the hero, or the same age—there are
no rules about that. But if you use a younger character, be careful
that she doesn't steal the book away from the hero (which is why
adult actors don't like performing with children). Or your hero may
be friends with an old man or woman, a popular device used in *The
Witch of Blackbird Pond*, by Elizabeth George Speare. But such
friendships have been overused in the past and are in danger of
being trite unless handled deftly. *See You Later, Crocodile*, by Geor-
gess McHargue, gives us a twist on old-woman-as-friend when the
old woman in question turns on the helpful hero and rejects her.
Two other potentially trite relationships are those with bullies and
tag-along little brothers or sisters; they must be handled with originality.

Your characters live in a place and a time, the choice of which
is up to you. Today's young readers prefer contemporary settings.
Sales show this again and again. But you are free to set your story
in the historical past, in a fantasy world, or in the future. One warn-
ing, however: don't set the story during the time *you* grew up or
name the characters after your friends. If the setting is only a generation ago, bring the story up to the present, and name your char-

acters after the children of your friends. Or look in the Births column in the newspaper to see which names are popular now. For each generation, the preceding one is old-fashioned, not quaint. Names that were trendy thirty years ago are stale today. Yes, the era when you grew up is endlessly enthralling—to you, and maybe to your grandchildren, but not to your children. Even if your children are an exception (do they often ask what was it like when Carter was president?), you may be sure other people's children are not—and they're the ones who will not read your book—nor will an editor, who is well aware of this sad but true fact.

Once you have decided on your characters, conflict, and setting, should you outline? Writers of nonfiction must outline, because of the difficulties in organizing factual material. If you're a beginning novelist, perhaps you should outline so that your goal will sustain you. Or you may simply feel more comfortable having every step pinned down in advance. Some writers prefer to choose a character and simply run with it, allowing themselves to be surprised as the story unfolds and new ideas come to them. Maybe one of the minor characters will cry out to become the protagonist; maybe this new character has an even more stimulating problem. The danger here is that one hundred pages later, you might realize you don't have a plot. It's a rare writer who knows everything about his book before it's done. Jerry Spinelli has said, "Sometimes I think writing is a performing rather than a fine art—almost a sport, in which you need confidence and spontaneity. Writing a book is like knowing I'm going to have to run from one end of the basketball court to the other to put the ball in the basket but not how I'm going to get there. You have to leave yourself enough freedom."

Plunge into your book. Begin your story *in media res*, in the middle of things. Richard Peck told me he always begins his books with dialog. This has been good advice for years (" 'Christmas won't be Christmas without any presents,' grumbled Jo, lying on the rug." *Little Women* by Louisa May Alcott). Or begin with action ("Nita slipped out the back door of the beach house. . . ." *Deep Wizardry* by Diane Duane), or with a sense of impending action or revelation ("Alice was beginning to get very tired of sitting by her sister on the bank. . . ." *Alice's Adventures in Wonderland* by Lewis Carroll). Openings like this make the reader want to continue reading. The first sentence is probably the most important one in the book because many readers, before committing themselves to spending hours with a book, will read that first sentence or first paragraph. If you've begun with an uninteresting description of a character or place, you'll probably lose that reader in under thirty seconds. And if an editor is tired or in a bad mood, you could lose her too.

When an editor is reading a submission, she knows it can take time for the writer to get to the point, and so she plows on (*if* she's in a good mood) through pages of tedious introductory material, looking for the point at which the book really begins. For example, many manuscripts begin with the hero waking up and thinking about the day ahead. Editors are aware that new writers tend to use the first chapter as a warm-up, taking this opportunity to describe characters and places, as if we'd never see them in action. When Hemingway asked F. Scott Fitzgerald for his opinion of the manuscript for *The Sun Also Rises*, Fitzgerald's only suggestion was that Hemingway throw away the first chapter, which he did. I've worked on dozens of manuscripts where I've said the same thing to the writers.

You don't need all that information in chapter 1. You've worked in personalities and descriptions as you went along in the book: you don't need to give us a guided tour in the beginning. Let events happen, and we'll come to know what we need to know gradually. Most editors will agree that superfluous first-chapter "introductions" are common faults in the manuscripts we receive.

Remember the six questions of journalism: Who? Where? When? What? How? Why? Answer as many as you can as soon as you can. Isn't it a marvel how writers can set the scene in a page or less? Pick up some books at random and study their first pages. See how the opening sentences cited above begin the job. Barbara Cartland is a whiz at fast setup, but, then, she's had a lot of practice. Don't try to work to a formula when setting up because that will sound clichéd to your readers. The information should come out naturally—even though you've worked hours to achieve that effect. Once you've got your opening pages in place, the rest of the book should flow along, because you've found your voice. Carroll was in Alice's head when he wrote that first sentence, even though he was writing *about* her. Some writers write the first chapter last, since they have a better idea of their book after it is finished. Robert Kimmel Smith has said that he once spent two months and sixty pages writing a novel—before he got to the beginning.

The opening chapter leads logically to the big event as the writer develops characters, "plants," and foreshadows. Leon Garfield once told me, "Beginnings and endings are easy. It's the middle that's most difficult for me." If you outlined, you may have already been alerted to the "slack middle" problem and conquered it.

Another way to prevent a slack middle is to delay important action until several set-up chapters are done. "In my first novel," the mystery writer Robert Barnard told me, "I had a murder in the first chapter. Then I had to keep killing people to sustain the action. Now I postpone the murder till the fourth or fifth chapter and don't have so many bodies lying about." Lois Duncan echoed Barnard when she said, "The big event usually takes place in about the fifth chapter. Before that, small events are building up to it. After that, I'm trying to resolve it."

What is the writer to do before the big event in the fifth or sixth chapter? Introduce the characters, of course, and begin plotting, planting, and foreshadowing. This is also where you can begin your subplot. A subplot adds texture to your book; this is the way most sitcoms are laid out, and the formula works well for novels, provided your characters and subplots are handled with subtlety. Take another look at your book idea: What are the possibilities for a subplot? Weave one in, remembering that not all problems have to be solved in books; simply addressing yourself and the reader to them may be enough. Subplots must evolve naturally from your material, otherwise the result will be as mechanical as an episode from a sitcom.

In *Me, Mop, and the Moondance Kid,* by Walter Dean Myers, T.J. and his younger brother Moondance, recently adopted, want to find a home for their pal Mop, who was left behind at the orphanage, which is going to close soon, which means that Mop will be sent far away. Mop has it all worked out: if she plays on the local Little League team, she's sure the coaches, a married couple, who may be scouting her for adoption, will want her to join their family. Note that Myers has set a deadline; this lends a sense of urgency to the action.

The subplot has to do with T.J. He'd always wanted a father who'd play ball with him, but now that he has one, T.J. can no longer hide the fact that he can't hit, catch, or throw—and that Moondance is a better player than he is.

By the end of the book, the coaches have adopted Mop, but T.J. is still a rotten ballplayer. However, says his father, if there were a trophy for the Most Improved Player, T.J. would have won it. In other words, no miracle appears for T.J., but the book has a happy ending not only for the characters but for the readers as well.

Fortunately for writers, life is full of problems because everyone wants something hard to get. Before you even start to write, ask yourself what *each* of your characters wants. For example, in *Little Women*, Beth wanted to be healthy, Amy wanted to be elegant, Meg wanted to marry, and Jo wanted to write. As for Laurie, he wanted friends, and Marmee wanted her husband home safe from the war. A book moves on wants—and particular wants determine the course of a book, as it does our lives. Writers were the first psychologists, and the best have the ability to understand people and the reasons for their behavior. Robert Kimmel Smith has said that his books are about "a person who struggles against overwhelming odds to achieve a worthwhile goal."

What do children want? The same things you and your peers wanted when you were young. Smith has listed some of the concerns of children as follows:

1. They want acceptance by their peers.
2. They worry about their position in the family, and how the family functions.
3. They are concerned about their physical growth: their size, puberty, their looks.
4. They are striving for a positive self-image, their own view of themselves.
5. They wonder what the future will hold, their own and that of their society and the world.

Change the clothes, change the music, change what's on the news, but kids are pretty much the same. When you've decided what your characters want and are striving for, you have the conflict that propels your book. Alice Bach told me that she uses the emotions she has today regarding current events in her life and gives them to younger characters. Trust yourself. You can write your book any want you want to, and no one has to see it until it's ready to be shown. Don't be afraid of freedom, because your best writing will come only if you dare to say what you feel.

6 Growing Up in the Malls

THROUGHOUT THIS BOOK I've spoken about the young adult novel, which many say began with *The Catcher in the Rye*. I'm not so sure about that. As a teenager in the 1950s I went to my local library and checked out books by Betty Cavanna, Mary Stolz, Maureen Daly, and others who wrote for and about teenagers. I also read Nancy Drew and all the titles in the Sue Barton, Student Nurse, series. As a member of the Scholastic Teen-Age Book Club, I bought paperback editions of such books as *Animal Farm* by George Orwell and *Andersonville* by MacKinlay Kantor. I also read the adult books you were supposed to keep a secret from your parents (*The Amboy Dukes*, *Tobacco Road*). I never heard the term "young adult" and had no idea it meant a book written for adults that was also suitable for teenagers. "Suitable" meant that it was "clean" and could be used for a book report. Kids in high school still read books like these: *The Old Man and the Sea*, *Lord of the Flies*, *Of Mice and Men*.

To publishers, the YA was a book about teenagers, and it, too, was clean. Then, in the late sixties and early seventies, the YA as we know it sprang into being with books like *The Pigman*, *The Outsiders*, and *The Cat Ate My Gymsuit*. Timely, hard-hitting, contemporary books like these for teenagers hit their stride in the 1970s. Every "problem" imaginable (what Robert Lipsyte has called the Big Ds: death, divorce, disease, and drugs) found itself in a YA book. This was the time of "consciousness-raising," and writers were free to use frank language and to write about almost anything they wished. YA books were no longer unrealistically scrubbed of sexual behavior among teenagers. In addition, publishers encouraged Hispanic, Asian American, and African American writers, who had long been underrepresented on their lists. Writers like Rosa Guy, Virginia Hamilton, Laurence Yep, Sharon Bell Mathis, Walter Dean Myers, and Nicholasa Mohr spoke directly to teen-agers of every background.

For the teacher, the new YA books were a godsend. Since they were reviewed well in the library and educational media, since they were shorter and easier to read than the YAs originally written for adults, and since they were about contemporary life, even reluctant readers could write book reports on them. During the years when the literacy level in the United States was declining, a young gen-eration of librarians and teachers embraced these books; they were "relevant."

Sold through the new, impersonal chain bookstores in the malls—where kids were already hanging out—these books filled a need. Teenagers with disposable income began buying their own books, books about people like themselves from salespeople who did not know their parents or teachers. By reflecting society as it really was, the YA had begun to grow up.

By the late seventies the YA was "hot." Publishers of paperback books paid hardcover houses high five-figure amounts for reprint rights to YAs by M. E. Kerr, Paul Zindel, Robert Cormier, and others. Delacorte Press, the hardcover arm of Dell Publishing, was especially strong in this field already, and had signed up YA authors like Norma Fox Mazer, Harry Mazer, and Paula Danziger, whom it was profitably publishing first in hardcover, then in Laurel-Leaf paper editions. Paperbacks made the YA more profitable for writers and publishers than ever before. They also led the way toward changing children's publishing from a snug cottage industry to big business.

Since the story of modern YA publishing is virtually contem-poraneous with the rise of paperbacks for young people, let me step back a bit and talk about the history of paperback publishing in the United States—an industry that is still young, growing, and chang-ing—especially in children's books.

Many think paperbacks are synonymous with "mass market." But, as George Nicholson, Vice President and Publisher at Dell Publishing, has often said, "Mass market refers only to *how* books are distributed and is often used in contrast to the word 'trade,' not as a description of quality of content." (Trade books are those you will find in bookstores. Some are hardcover, some are paperback.

They are not textbooks, which have yet another distribution system.)

The term "mass market" was coined in the early days of paperback publishing, when cheap, paperbound editions of books were sold through newsstands rather than through bookstores. By the time of the Great Depression, a number of paperback publishers had been established, with varying degrees of success. The first modern line in the United States was Pocket Books, which was only partially owned by Simon & Schuster then. One of their most famous books was *Bambi* by Felix Salten.

The first Bantam Books entered the marketplace in 1945, in direct competition with Dell and Pocket Books. Bantam, however, had the high-powered backing of the Curtis Publishing Corporation, publishers of the prestigious and successful magazines *The Saturday Evening Post* and *The Ladies' Home Journal*. Bantam was also backed by Grosset & Dunlap, which was then a hardcover reprint house that had been acquired by a consortium of leading trade publishers (Random House, Harpers, Scribner's, and Little, Brown).

The legendary Ian Ballantine, who had been associated with the American division of Penguin Books, founded Bantam with Oscar Dystel and soon signed up writers like Hemingway, Steinbeck, and Fitzgerald (who had been published by Penguin during the war). Ballantine was following the example of Allen Lane, who had begun the Penguin line in England in 1935. Readers by the millions were thrilled to buy books of such caliber for only a quarter. For their part, the writers were happy to be reaching so many readers, since Penguin U.S.A. had never had the mass distribution Bantam has become known for.

In 1952 Ballantine left Bantam and founded Ballantine Books. Under Dystel in the 1950s and 1960s, Bantam went on to become the dominant literary paperback publisher. Bantam not only had wholesalers and newsstand distribution, it also developed a *separate* sales force that sold to independent trade bookstores (there were almost no major chains then). *This was the first time mass-market paperbacks entered trade bookstores along with hardcovers.* Bantam, combined with Dell, remains the largest paperback publisher in the United States, followed by Pocket Books, Avon, and New American Library.

Founded by George Delacorte in 1921, Dell had begun publishing paperbacks (mysteries, westerns, romances) in 1943. The first reps who sold paperbacks were the same people who had sold magazines to the newsstands. In the 1940s and 1950s, for example, Dell was still famous for its comic books and for crossword puzzle and astrology magazines. *In 1963 Dell became the first paperback publisher to set up its own hardcover line, Delacorte Press.* Major writers like James Jones and Irwin Shaw signed "hard/soft deals" with Delacorte/Dell. Delacorte paid a generous advance to the writer, who kept the entire amount rather than splitting it with his hardcover publisher.

Delacorte Press also began publishing hardcover titles for young people, which, like the adult titles, went into paperback editions a year or so later. In this way, Dell could obtain reprint rights for less than if a different hardcover publisher had been involved, since the writer was no longer giving up a percentage of the money. Again, this innovation pleased the publisher and the writer. The reader ignored it, since most readers care nothing about who publishes which books.

Carl W. "Bud" Tobey, a former president of Dell, once told me, "One of the most frustrating things in this business is that the consumer doesn't give a damn who published a book. He never goes into a bookstore and asks, 'Do you have the latest Dell or Avon book?' He asks instead, 'Do you have the latest Ludlum or Steel?' We spend loads of money to acquire, produce, and advertise books, and no one even knows our name.' " Although there's a great deal of truth in Tobey's statement, it doesn't always apply to children's paperbacks.

In 1965, encouraged by the high sales of comic books to children, Helen Meyer, president of Dell, believed the same distribution system could handle children's books. A year later Dell, under George Nicholson, introduced the Yearling line of exceptional children's books, with such titles as *Charlotte's Web* by E. B. White and the Newbery Medal–winner *Johnny Tremain* by Esther Forbes. Dell had already launched the Laurel-Leaf imprint, which specialized in young adult titles.

The economic doldrums of the 1970s brought about major changes in publishing books for children; since library funds had dwindled, publishers had to find ways to enter the bookstore market in greater numbers than before. Pop-up books for the youngest readers were one answer. Paperbacks for teenagers were another.

In 1974, S. E. Hinton offered her new book, *Rumble Fish*, to Viking, her original hardcover publisher. Her agent believed she deserved a good advance for it, justified by the sales of her two previous novels, *The Outsiders* and *That Was Then, This Is Now*. But money was tight in those years, and the sum she asked for was too large for a children's book, Viking said. Although Hinton did not want to leave her original publisher, after much soul-searching she took *Rumble Fish* to Ron Buehl at Dell, her paperback publisher, and she has remained there ever since. Besides *Rumble Fish*, Delacorte Press later published her fourth and fifth novels, *Tex* and *Taming the Star Runner*, in hardcover.

Around the same time Buehl paid Morrow an unprecedented $1,100,000 for the reprint rights to eighteen backlist titles by Beverly Cleary, including her highly successful Ramona books. Children's publishing—especially on the paperback side—was becoming Big Business.

All over town editors heard the news and recollected how much they had enjoyed series books when they were young. Most series books had been available only at the five-and-ten and in people's cellars; very few could be found in libraries. Cleary had never forgotten that children love to read about the same characters in new adventures. Was someone out there who could become the next Beverly Cleary?

Patricia Reilly Giff, it turned out, had two novels under consideration at Viking. With the news of the Cleary sale still ringing in my ears, I went into Nicholson, who was then editorial director, and said, "We've got two humorous novels by an unpublished writer. If we publish just one, as a first novel, it's going to get lost. Why don't we ask Pat to take these two books, which are about different characters, and rewrite them as a series?" Since the word "series" was still suspect, we called these two books (*Fourth-Grade Celebrity* and *The Girl Who Knew It All*) "companion novels." As the seventies drew to a close, Nicholson and I left Viking for Delacorte, where we published Giff's two books as "The Adventures of Casey Valentine and Her Friends" in the fall of 1979. But this was only a modest effort, compared with what was to come.

Series publishing was reborn in the eighties, coinciding with the publishers' need to generate more sales in the bookstores and with the outstanding growth of paperback outlets, such as newsstands in airports, supermarkets, libraries, and in neighborhoods where no other kind of book is ever sold.

And now, Enter the Packager, or Book Producer. Dan Weiss,

formerly an editor for Golden Press, Scholastic, and Simon & Schuster, also felt the winds of change and, with his brother Jeff, founded Cloverdale Press. What did teenagers want? they asked. Romance, came the answer. And so the best-selling Bantam series Sweet Dreams was born, inspired by the success of the Wildfire line at Scholastic. Sweet Dreams became number one on B. Dalton's best-seller list in 1982. Other paperback publishers jumped on the lovewagon with their own romance lines:

POCKET BOOKS: First Love
BERKELEY: Caprice
WARNER: Two by Two; Make Your Dreams Come True Romances
NEW AMERICAN LIBRARY: Magic Moments; Turning Points

Several publishers, like Avon (Flare), Pacer (Two Hearts), and Dell (Young Love) resisted the lure of formula romance publishing and began to issue, disguised as romance lines, solid love stories by well-known writers such as Madeleine L'Engle, Richard Peck, and Norma Fox Mazer.

Romance swept away the entire category of hi/lo books (high interest/low reading level) for reluctant readers. Nonfiction for teenagers had never sold well in paperback; it, too, died, after ailing since the 1970s. Sales of literary novels ("midlist books") and historical fiction began to decline. The problem novel lost ground as the mood of the country became conservative and escapist. The Council on Interracial Books for Children called romance novels "a backsliding, a regression to the most sexist messages of the 1940s and 1950s. . . ." Few preteen and teen readers heeded this appeal.

Surveying the phenomenal growth of series and romance novels, *Publishers Weekly* proclaimed in its October 19, 1984, issue: "For those who can catch the right tone for today's teenagers, this is the hot new area in publishing."

Hardcover publishers, with their small staffs, continued to publish good books. Still committed to the serious YA, Delacorte Press established a contest for an outstanding first young adult novel. At the same time, paperback publishers struggled to keep up with the demand for escapist teen fantasies by turning to packagers.

The oldest packagers for children—Stratemeyer (Nancy Drew/Hardy Boys), beginning in 1906; Zokeisha (Chubby Board Books), 1950s; and Porter Productions (Stretch Books), 1945—had been joined by a dozen new ones by 1986. Judy Gitenstein, editorial director at Bantam Books for Young Readers, told Ann Martin in *Publishers Weekly*, "Packagers save editors and publishers time on all levels. . . . Using packagers is one way of adding to the department." Packagers came up with ideas for series, hired writers, edited the manuscripts, and sometimes assigned cover art and arranged for the printing and binding of the finished book. Preeminent among the YA packagers were Cloverdale Press, Mega-Books, Inc., Parachute Press, and the Philip Lief Group, Inc.

After the success of the romance lines, it was clear that packaged series could help publishers maintain a strong hold on teenage buyers in the chain bookstores. Jean Feiwel, vice president and editorial director at Scholastic, said that teenage romances made up about 40 percent of the YA book market in 1984. That same year, in the *Wilson Library Bulletin*, Patty Campbell, a long-time supporter of YA books, told librarians: "Excellent YA fiction and nonfiction are still being written and published. But it is all beginning to seem alarmingly anachronistic."

In addition to romances, packagers supplied books in other categories such as "reader participation" (the many imitations of Choose Your Own Adventure); speculative fiction reader participation (Fighting Fantasy Gamebooks and others); horror (Twilight, Dark Forces); mysteries (Diana Winthrop and others); action-adventure (Race Against Time); and theme series (Electric High; the Zodiac Club).

The love affair with packagers began to cool somewhat by the late eighties. Many publishers who had lost a great deal of money purchasing and promoting series that sold poorly grew cautious. After the market became glutted, romance lines thinned out. In-house editors like Jean Feiwel found it could be highly profitable to suggest a concept, like the Babysitters Club, to a writer like Ann M. Martin. For their part, writers learned to propose their own series to editors, as David Adler had done with Cam Jensen. And like Francine Pascal (Sweet Valley High), a writer could also create a series with a packager, who would then sell it to a publisher. How can publishers resist the lure of series, especially when they see the huge corporate banner waving the words "Bottom Line"!

Although you can propose a series to an editor, if you are not an experienced writer, your chance of selling an idea is slim. You can get the experience by writing for packagers first, which is a good way to break into series publishing. You can obtain a list of children's book packagers and other information from the American Book Producers Association. You can also get a detailed list of publishers and packagers in the *Novel & Short Story Writer's Market* annual, published by Writer's Digest Books.

In the 1990 edition, Ellen Steiber of Cloverdale Press stated: "We work very closely with our writers, much more closely than do editors at publishing houses." Since the packager usually has a publishing client and a series concept in place before the writers are hired, you will receive a great deal of direction. Payment is usually on a work-for-hire basis, with the writer receiving a flat fee and no royalties. Your work may appear under the pseudonym chosen for a series, and you usually give up *all* rights to the work. On the other hand, packagers are willing to give new writers a chance. Under the intense editorial direction, writers can learn a great deal about plotting, pacing, and the other elements of writing a novel. Robin Hardy, a former editor at Cloverdale, and now with Dan Weiss Associates, says, "Snappy dialogue, good repartee, and realistic slang" catch his attention. Books from packagers must be *au courant*, because series readers demand contemporaneity.

Series can run from a few books to a hundred or more, depending on their success. Packagers provide writers with a "bible," describing the characters, setting, and story line, along with copies of previous books in the series, which the writer must read. The needs of individual packagers differ, but if you would like to try writing for one, by all means send in writing samples. If you have an idea of your own for a series, you can send it in, with some plot outlines and a few chapters, to either a packager or a publisher.

Nowadays, both trade and mass-market editors are publishing series, although they differ in kind and in the rate at which the books are published. Hardcover houses emphasize quality: good writing and strong characterization. Writers retain rights to their material, and receive advances, royalties, and a share of subsidiary rights. Mass-market houses and packagers say that "concept is everything." Since the books are heavily promoted and appear in the bookstores at the rate of one a month or so, strict deadlines must be kept. Being the sole writer of a series is grueling, but if the series is a success, the financial rewards are great.

Packagers continue to fill a need—Mega-Books hires the writers for all the Nancy Drew, Hardy Boys, and Bobbsey Twins series for

Pocket Books, for example. Series continue to be published, though the emphasis at present is on books for younger readers. Mass-market houses may need them more than ever because of a new trend in paperback publishing, which has resulted in fewer books being available for reprinting.

One hardcover house after another has now either strengthened its existing paperback lines or begun new ones. Many no longer offer their hardcover books to the mass-market houses; when the terms of license become "vulnerable," or up for renewal, they reclaim the titles for their own paperback lines. Morrow, for example, did not renew the ten-year license for the Beverly Cleary titles Buehl had purchased. Her books are now published by Avon, which, like Morrow, is part of the Hearst Corporation. As the flow of books from hardcover houses dried up, some mass-market houses began to publish hardcovers in self-defense.

These changes raise some important considerations for writers. A writer who has published with three different hardcover houses, say, may find herself published by three different paperback lines instead of the one who used to buy all her reprint rights. How much "extra" are her publishers offering for a hard/soft deal? Will the writer earn as much money if her book is not offered to one of the big mass-market reprint houses? Does she have any say about where she wants the paperbacks of her books to be published? Will her books be promoted consistently when they are spread around so many different publishers? One thing is clear: Children's publishing has become more like adult publishing, as editors vie for major authors, holding out big advances and hard/soft deals as inducements.

You may be wondering how to get your book published in paperback. You can offer it to some paperback houses directly, but the usual way is to get it published first in a hardcover edition. If your publisher has a paperback line, as in the case of Delacorte/Dell, Viking/Puffin, Knopf/Random House, it will buy hard/soft rights, meaning it is buying the paperback rights at the same time as the hardcover rights.

If the publisher has no paperback line, as in the case of Holiday House, it will publish the book in hardcover and will later offer the book to paperback publishers, or reprint houses, who seem likely purchasers. Some of the largest hardcover houses, like Macmillan, hold rights conferences where mass-market paperback editors convene to hear presentations of the titles. (Even though Macmillan has a paperback line it cannot accommodate all the books it publishes in its many imprints and offers some to the mass-market houses.)

At other houses, the subsidiary rights manager will send the books to the mass-market houses. She has taken note of special circumstances, as, for example, whether a particular publisher has published the writer before or has an option on her next work.

Occasionally a novel will stand out to such an extent that the hardcover publisher will announce an auction. Copies of the book will go to paperback houses with a letter informing the editors that an auction will be held on a specific date. Sometimes the publisher will set a "floor" in advance, which means he will not consider offers for the book that are under a specified amount. Reprint houses will read the book and telephone their offers. Sometimes the high bidder will set the floor and get "topping" privileges. The subsidiary rights manager will tell the other bidders what the highest offer was but will not reveal who made it. The other houses will have another chance to bid. This may go on for several rounds of bidding. Finally, the original high bidder will decide whether to take advantage of the topping privilege, which must exceed a certain percentage of the highest bid from the last round.

Let us say three paperback houses, Aye, Bee, and Cee, have decided to participate in Bench Press's auction of the paperback rights to your novel, *Eating Dogfood Is No Fun*. During the first round of bidding, Bee offers the earliest and highest bid, $15,000, and earns the topping privilege, in this case, 10 percent. The bidding continues. During the last round Aye makes a final offer of $30,000 and Cee offers $31,000. Now, as holder of the floor, Bee must decide whether to drop out or to top the $31,000 by $3,100 (10 percent) for a total of $34,100. If Bee declines to top, Cee will get the book.

During an auction a frenzy seems to come over the participants as they vie for a book; it's an exciting time, and if the money is big enough, it will make news, which in turn may enhance the sales potential of the book. On the other hand, sometimes a publisher will announce an auction but nobody will make a bid. This can be embarrassing.

Usually sales are conducted more quietly. Reprint editors read the submissions from the hardcover houses, select a few, and make offers ranging from about $3,000 up, along with a standard schedule of royalties. The author usually receives 50 percent of the offer, and the publisher retains the other half. This may not seem fair, but it should be kept in mind that the hardcover house discovered the author, did the editing and promoting, and as a consequence, is entitled to a good share of the income.

If you don't feel like sharing the income in this way, the next time you write a book you might want to try to sell it to a house with its own paperback line. You will receive a slightly higher initial advance than you would for a hardcover-only sale, and you will keep all the royalties. But there is no guarantee that the publisher will ever issue your book in paperback, and he may not offer the book to another paperback house!

The rise of blockbuster paperback series led to their replacing the standard YA in the chain bookstores. This, combined with the loss of funds for YA collections in the libraries and the increase in the population of younger children, meant that by 1990 the young adult market was extremely soft. Established nonseries, nonformula YA writers were lamenting their royalty statements. Editors advised them to write for younger readers while waiting for their audience to grow older.

Was it only six years earlier that *Publishers Weekly* had called YA "the hot new area in publishing"? Will the coming generation of teenagers spurn books entirely in favor of "general entertainment such as talking on the telephone and watching videos?" asked Beverly Horowitz, editorial director of the Bantam Starfire line. Will teenagers jump straight from middle-grade fiction to James Clavell and Mary Higgins Clark? Will young adult publishing become extinct? The answer is of concern to writers.

YA books will rise from the ashes, and they will be better than ever. Helene Steinhauer, managing editor of Dell Books for Young Readers, remembers that in 1978 she noticed the Yearling schedule had very few books on it while Laurel-Leaf was full. Ten years later it was just the opposite. "YA will be back," she says. "Today's Yearling readers will be tomorrow's Laurel-Leaf readers, and another cycle will begin."

Teenagers, by definition self-absorbed, will always want to read about themselves. Hot trend gives way to hot trend, but what remains—always—is the good story, written from the writer's heart, reflecting his deep interest in a subject. It's the writer, not the publisher, who sets the trend, and we must never forget that. Young adult books are coming of age, along with their readers. In addition to the young readers waiting for adolescence to strike, there's a new audience already out there for YA.

Writing in the SCBW *Bulletin*, Marion Markham observed that women in their early twenties are reading YAs. In many areas the YA books are now shelved in the adult sections of libraries. One librarian said, "It was too confusing—Joan Lowery Nixon was on the same shelf as *Dubliners* in the YA section, because *Dubliners* was required reading. But adults who wanted *Dubliners* couldn't find it." Markham also said that adults are seeking alternatives to mindless romances and to Stephen King (as one said, "I couldn't finish one of his books because of the awful gore"). Teenage books remind young mothers and other working women of their carefree days, and they've had enough of "five-hundred-page epics about international cartels, enough of reading about the problems of fantasy-world millionaires." But mostly it's because, as one woman said, "If a book has a good plot and good characters, does it matter whether it's for adults or young adults?" Another unlikely audience for the YA are senior citizens, who've long enjoyed them.

Catherine Clancy of the Boston Public Library told me recently that teenagers are coming in and asking for serious books about young adults. "Not problem novels," she said, "but novels with substance." The last few years have seen some remarkable books, unlike any published before for teenagers, from Peter Dickinson's *Eva* to Robert Cormier's *Fade*. The writing is professional, the subject matter diverse. Could this be the start of a trend?

"Let us dig in and wait it out," said Patty Campbell in her 1984 article. "At regular intervals during the past century one 'trash' series after another has risen on a wave of popularity and canny merchandising, swept past teachers and librarians who viewed [them] with alarm, and ebbed away in a few years to leave not ruined lives but only a pleasant residue of nostalgia."

7 Writer, Edit Yourself

HOW MANY TIMES have I seen promising manuscripts marred by simple faults the writers should have corrected before sending them out? It's not enough to write: you must write carefully, and you must line-edit your work. Claire Smith, a literary agent, told me, "When I begin to read a manuscript and see on the first page that the writer doesn't know the difference between 'its' and 'it's,' I stop reading. I don't have time to spend on people who don't know the basics."

We all have some bad writing habits and blind spots about grammar and spelling, and sometimes we're not sure if we're doing the right thing. If you know you're not a good speller and your knowledge of grammar is a bit shaky, ask a friend to proofread your work or offer to pay a high-school English teacher to go over your manuscript. First impressions count.

In more leisurely days, editors and agents were more patient with writers who couldn't spell, but in today's hurried world, if you are trying to get your first or second book published, sloppy work may doom you from the start. Would you pay full price for a brand-new car that had dents in it? Likewise, would an editor be impressed by a manuscript that was full of flaws?

So much poor writing gets published that we may come to think that it's acceptable. Not all editors are literate, but those who are will send the manuscript back to you, even if you've written a good story, because they haven't time to line-edit your work or give you a writing lesson. Learning the craft of writing will not automatically make your work salable, but it can help. The art of writing is something you know intuitively, and it is nurtured by reading the best, including plays and poetry. But neither genius nor talent is enough if you haven't mastered your craft.

Let's assume that you've written *Eating Dogfood Is No Fun*. Remember the story? Jennifer Scrimshaw has learned that her parents are getting a divorce, and her little brother, Elvis, has run away from home and been missing for a night. With the help of a classmate, Rodney, Jennifer finds Elvis. He stayed overnight in an empty summer cottage, and her heart nearly breaks when she sees he's survived on canned dogfood. When she and Elvis return home, they have a showdown with their parents, who've refused to talk about the divorce to the children. As a subplot, during the hunt for Elvis, Jennifer and Rodney get to know each other—and it looks as if they'll stay friends.

This scenario could work for a middle-grade or young adult novel, depending on Jennifer's age and on what the characters do. For example, if Jennifer and Rodney find Elvis by riding around on their bicycles, this is most likely a middle-grade novel. If Rodney drives Jennifer around in his car, it's a YA. If Jennifer drinks milk and Coke, it's a middle-grade. If Jennifer drinks beer and snorts coke, it's a YA.

At all events, it's finished! All ready to send to Annabelle Jones at the famous publishing house, Bench Press. But is it? You've been so close to this book for so long, your vision of it has suffered. You are satisfied with your characters, who are well-rounded. The plot and subplot move smoothly. What more can you do? As far as you're concerned, it's ready to mail.

Wait a day or so until your excitement abates. Then go over your manuscript with a cool eye for your writing style. The problems listed below are ones I find recurring in contemporary writing; the list is by no means complete, but it's a good start.

Does each scene and incident in the book advance either the plot or the characterization? What about that scene where Jennifer and Rodney talk about their favorite ice cream flavors? Are they revealing nuances of character? Or are you filling up space on the page, where you didn't know what else to say? Be sure you're not going off on tangents, an especially common problem in first-person YA. You can write forever about nonessentials to avoid dealing with your characters. In the heat of composition, everything seems relevant to the book, and the temptation to throw it all in is great—especially for writers with word processors. Dispensing with the irrelevant is probably the severest test of your objectivity. Hard-hearted as you may be, it's a rare writer who cuts all the beloved irrelevancies and tangents; a good editor will do the rest, provided you've not so bored him that he refuses to finish reading your book.

Throughout, are you showing or telling? *Effective writing depends on showing through action, dialog, or detail.* For example,

> "Jennifer felt dismayed. The rain had wiped out Elvis's footprints. Since his trail had ended, she didn't know what to do next."

This is telling. You've told us how Jennifer felt. You've told us the trail had ended. And you've told us she was at a loss. Compare this with:

> "Jennifer stood in the rain, staring at the dirt turning into mud. Elvis's footprints were gone."

This shows us how she felt. The "dirt turning into mud" also shows that her hope had turned into despair. The statement about the footprints is telling, but the finality of the sentence also conveys how she felt. We are "inside" Jennifer, feeling what she's feeling, and we understand that she doesn't know what to do next; you don't have to tell us. Don't think that children need everything spelled out. Spelling out every nuance leaves little for the reader to imagine. Let the "showing" do the work and don't tell the reader what to think or feel. If you wrote your manuscript on a word processor, program it to find every use of "felt." Then examine each sentence: are you telling instead of showing? Or take a highlighter and mark each use. You may have more work to do, after all.

Many writers tend to give complete descriptions of what people are wearing. Again, this is usually to fill up space, and few readers will remember a description like this:

> When Jennifer first saw Rodney, he was wearing distressed jeans and a blue-and-white checked flannel shirt under a blue parka, which was unzipped. He had short, brown, curly hair and blue eyes. On his feet he had clean, white Reeboks and navy blue socks.

We've learned that Rodney is fashionably dressed for cool weather in the early 1990s, and is good at coordinating colors. But what have we learned about his *character*? Clothing should be mentioned only if it's a clue to character or has some other function in the story, such as a costume at Halloween. And if it's mentioned at all, the mention should be brief.

"Jennifer peered through the window of the cottage. Elvis, in only a T-shirt and jeans, was eating."

Since it's been established (by Rodney's clothes) that the weather is chilly, Elvis's clothes indicate that his running away was unplanned; they also make us feel sorry for him because he's got to be cold.

"It is the details that give a book its richness," Joan Aiken once told me. And it is her choice of detail that keeps her books so vivid that if I put one down, I'm compelled to pick it up again. Hers are details that count, adding color, texture, life—and, above all, meaning. Tedious lists of what people are wearing or eating or thinking blur the effect. John O'Hara once wrote that he strove to find the exact detail, such as the kind of shirt collar a man wore, that would tell the reader all he needed to know about a character. What do you learn about the Scrimshaws from the following list?

Mrs. Scrimshaw's hair was in curlers.
Grease was embedded under Mr. Scrimshaw's nails.
Jennifer couldn't finish her TV dinner.

I often think every writer should take a playwriting course to learn how to write dialog so that it fits the characters and moves the action along. *Each character should sound like himself,* but be on the alert for caricatures and stereotypes. It's a rare thirty-year-old father who will routinely address his son as "young man." Stick to standard English. Don't try to keep up with the latest slang or vogue words, because by the time the book is published the slang will be outdated. One word of slang will give away a book's publication date. Did the boy say "moolah," "bucks," "dough," "brass," or "bread"? Did the girl say the boy was a "jerk," a "creep," a "nerd," a "dwebe," a "wimp," a "wuss," "a dork," a "weenie"? Use the wrong word, and your credibility as a writer for contemporary children is lost.

Some slang ("guy," "kid," "cool," "gross") has passed into the language and become almost legitimate, but when you're trying to be current, you can't know whether the latest slang will become standard, so it's best to avoid it. Lively writing does not depend on slang. It depends on how you use the English language. The same holds true for current events, from movies to rock concerts to election campaigns. *Write for the long term*, because your book may be in print for years. Ten or fifteen years down the line, a new "generation" may be reading your book, and if they find it dated, it will not continue to stay in print. If you must use a real name, when referring to popular culture, find one you believe will be around for a long time. Fortunately, with the rise of the VCR, movies like *E. T.* or *The Little Mermaid* or *The Wizard of Oz* have this kind of staying power. But few teenagers care who Bob Dylan is. Time moves fast in these mass-media days, so be selective.

When writing dialog, pay attention to the *verbs of speech*. "Said" is usually the best, along with "asked," and "answered." Then, too, there are the verbs indicating a certain kind of speech: "yelled," "bellowed," "whispered," "mumbled." Use these sparingly. Watch out for "hissed"; the sentence better be hissable, that is, have an *S* or two in it. " 'Elvis,' she hissed" is all right. " 'Rodney,' she hissed" is not.

Words to avoid include "reminded," "breathed," "demanded," "suggested," "laughed," and "lied": these are not verbs of speech. " 'I left a note,' lied Elvis" is not good; " 'I left a note,' said Elvis, lying" is better; but if we already know he's lying (which we do), why say it?

You need not use an adverb after a verb of speech because the dialog should convey the emotion. Writers of romances and series are usually telling their readers what to think, so they tack them on. In the late fifties, my friends and I played a game called Tom Swifty. Players had to come up with dialog followed by an adverb that was a play on words in the dialog. For example, " 'I love my new pool,' said Tom swimmingly," or " 'There's nothing on this paper,' said Tom blankly." This last came from Bill McCay, a former editor at Mega-Books and one of the writers for the Tom Swift series. His Tom uses many fewer adverbs than the old Tom used to. "But the new Tom still has some," he said swiftly, "because I can't always find a way to avoid them." Granted, but when I see a manuscript aswarm with adverbs after verbs of speech, I can't help but think, "Tom Swifties!" It's one of the first signs of a novice.

" 'We'll never find him,' said Jennifer disappointedly."

First, "disappointedly" is an awkward adverb; second, it's not needed. You could write:

" 'We'll never find him,' said Jennifer, disappointed."

But, again, why tell the reader how Jennifer felt? If the writing is good, the reader will know how she felt.

Don't be an intrusive author, editorializing for us. "Jennifer wisely decided to ask Rodney for help." That's your opinion, and it has no place in a book told from Jennifer's point of view.

Are you perfect? Of course not. Therefore, none of the characters in your book should be perfect, that is, one-dimensional. Although Jennifer is concerned about her family, she's also egocentric. Elvis tells her that he ran away because she, like their parents, was so involved in herself that she didn't take time to consider how he might be feeling. In formula fiction, characters are one-dimensional because that's what the readers want: a princess, a prince, and a rival. But good books show that people are complex. And plots grow out of their faults as well as their virtues. Take a hard look at each of your characters. Each one should have both good and bad traits. *The more human your characters, the more memorable they'll be.* Take an especially hard look at old people, small children, and villains! They are the easiest to stereotype.

Your choice of diction sets the tone of the book. In general, avoid excessive formality in books for children. A first- or third-person narrator should not use a big, Latinate word like "disorganized" when a shorter, Anglo-Saxon word like "mess" would do. If, however, formality is a trait of your character—go ahead and use it. A politician might talk about "negative impact not having a positive effect"; he's trying to impress someone. Watch out especially for words with -ion at the end. Too many of those, and your book will sound like an exam paper.

On the other hand, don't become too informal. For example, many people under forty say "Her mom . . ." That's becoming acceptable in dialog since it mirrors contemporary speech, but in third-person narration, say "her mother." Words we shorten in speech, like "bike," should be used in full form in third-person narrative.

"Jennifer grabbed her bicycle. 'I'm going to look for him on my bike,' she yelled."

Many words are trademarks and should be capitalized. It's Coke, Kleenex, Xerox copy, Windbreaker, Polaroid, Windsurfer,

Corn Flakes, Frisbee. Some writers are fond of using trade names for realism, which is fine, but are you sure you want to use your book as a vehicle for free commercials?

Vary your sentence structure. Does one sentence follow another in the same pattern: subject-verb, subject-verb? Now and then, begin a sentence with an adverbial phrase. A sentence fragment when it's appropriate. And why not throw in a question once in a while?

Too many novice writers regard punctuation as a necessary evil; on the contrary, it's a powerful tool when used correctly. (Some writers think the semicolon should not be used in children's books because it makes the writing look "too hard" and scares poor readers away. So the punctuation you use depends in part on the audience you wish to reach.)

It is so easy to fall into using the passive voice that you must *highlight each passive construction.* Put them into the active voice if you can. More than anything else, the passive voice makes nonfiction dull. Good writing is vivid. It's impossible to see an invisible agent, as in:

"A can of dogfood was placed on the table." (By whom?)

Wordiness is also death to vivid writing. "Omit needless words," advised Oliver Strunk in 1935. This is still excellent advice.

Jennifer was interested to see that there was a can of dogfood on the table.

Two short words that can kill vivid writing are "There is." Highlight there is/there are/there was/there were, etc., whenever they appear and try to think of ways to rephrase the statements, using verbs.

A can of dogfood *stood* on the table.

It's not always possible to eliminate "there is," which after all, is perfectly correct English. But change as many such constructions as you can by recasting the sentence.

Get rid of verbal clutter! Highlight and delete the following words when you can:

"Just," "really," "very," and "all" usually add no new information, and their omission often makes the statement stronger.

"Somehow." ("Somehow she knew Elvis was in the cottage."

No "somehow" about it. She knew intuitively, or she had good reasons for knowing.) The writer is too lazy to *think*. Watch out, too, for "something" and "thing," which are also vague. If the right word doesn't come to mind while you're writing, put in "thing" or "something" but don't leave it there when you're revising!

"Suddenly," "quickly," and other such adverbs, especially at the beginning of sentences, fail to convey speed because they slow down the reader, interfering with his getting to the all-important verb. ("Suddenly, she was falling." "Quickly, he ran out the door.")

Steer clear of vogue words like "incredible," "amazing," "awesome," "tremendous," and so on. Save these powerful words for the right occasion, such as a nuclear catastrophe or a visit to Niagara Falls.

"Literally" has lately come to be used as an emphatic. ("He was literally eating dogfood.") Not only is this incorrect (see your dictionary), it's far from vivid writing. Highlight it and be sure you're using it properly.

"Plus" is not a synonym for "and," as in "Plus she had to call Elvis's friends." This usage is incorrect and another vogue word. The same is true of "hopefully," used in place of "I hope." Although William Safire has said "hopefully" deserves to be standard usage since "everybody" is using it, the careful writer avoids it (except, perhaps, in dialog).

"Hopefully, Jennifer would find Elvis before dark" is poor writing; "hopefully" is an adverb and should modify a verb. "Jennifer searched hopefully for Elvis" is better, and even better is "Jennifer hoped she would find Elvis before dark." Do you see how vague "hopefully" is in the first sentence? Who is hoping? Even if you know that it's Jennifer, doesn't it sound weak? She's searching for her lost brother!

About twenty-five years ago, Jacques Barzun lamented the increasing use of the false possessive. A thing cannot possess another thing, he said. Now we routinely hear airline pilots say "New York's LaGuardia Airport . . ." and newscasters say "Pakistan's president." Where did this lazy usage come from? A journalist friend blames the space needs of reporters—they have to cram a lot of news into a small space, she says, and one way is to drop articles and prepositions. When the result is murkiness as in "Its lava's flow," from a science article about volcanoes on Venus, and flabby phrases (from an otherwise well-written novel) like "He got out of the boat and shoved its prow onto the beach"; "he walked up the garden's path"; and "stood in the archway's mouth," I begin to wonder whether he entered through the house's door. The possessive is vexing enough; why complicate its use in this way?

When I hear or read any of these usages, I wince as if I'd heard a wrong note played during a concert. Please don't cause unnecessary pain to your readers.

Use adjectives and adverbs sparingly. Every reader has ideal pictures of things. If I say "ball," you will see a particular kind of ball in your mind's eye. If I say "red ball," your picture will probably change. But if I put an adverb in front of the adjective, as in "a bright red ball," am I helping you see "my" ball better? "Red" is usually "bright." As in the description of Rodney above, too many words blur the picture rather than sharpen it.

Some writers worry about repeating nouns, including proper nouns, and will try to find other words in place of a name. One word for this is *periphrasis*, a term for using more words than are needed. Henry James was notorious for changing people's names to descriptions of them, which makes the New York edition of his works more difficult to read than the Penguin editions, which were published before James became so prolix.

> "Elvis scooped out another chunk of dogfood. The shivering boy put the material into his mouth."

Didn't you have to pause and think about the shivering boy, wondering where he came from and what the material was? Modern writers no longer use such circumlocutions; they simply use the proper name or a pronoun.

> "Elvis scooped out another chunk of dogfood. He put it in his mouth."

Start a notebook of verbs. Flat writing is the result of using tired verbs, along with all the faults listed above. How many English words do you know (and use) for motion? Here's a sampling of words meaning motion on foot, only: walk, run, trot, plod, jog, wander, sashay, trudge, truck, lope, race, dash, dart, poke along, glide, slide, stumble, and many more, each with its own *specific* meaning. To avoid monotony, to convey different kinds of action, to move your work along, you need verbs, especially for the simple, repeated actions like moving from one place to another. Choose among them and know how to use each word precisely. You should own a copy of *Webster's New Dictionary of Synonyms,* which, unlike a thesaurus, discriminates between synonyms and will tell you, for example, the subtle difference between "saunter" and "meander," both of which imply aimless movement. Good writers love verbs!

Another point about verbs: Use verbs, not participles ending in -ing, when trying to convey separate, *consecutive* actions. For example,

> "Jennifer ran for her bicycle, jumped on it, and rode off" instead of "Running for her bicycle, Jennifer jumped on it and rode off." (A good trick if she can do it!)

Such participles should be used only with *simultaneous* actions:

> "Looking at his watch, Rodney said, 'We'd better hurry.' "

It's not always possible to think of all of this during the heat of creation. Your first task is to get your thoughts down. Once the manuscript is finished, however, become your own line editor. You'll find many good books on writing at the library, including books on usage. Most writers swear by *The Elements of Style* by William Strunk, Jr.; it's full of good advice not only from Strunk but also from E. B. White. Every writer should own a copy. Copy editors and proofreaders refer to *Words into Type* or *The Chicago Manual of Style* for matters of punctuation and grammar. It wouldn't hurt if writers also had these books at the ready, to understand why copy editors have made certain changes. When it comes to contemporary usage, you're on your own, since even the experts disagree on many points. A good starting place is Fowler's *Modern English Usage,* Wilson Follett's *Modern American Usage,* and *Webster's Dictionary of English Usage.* These books are fun to browse through. You will also learn a great deal about our language and will see how it has changed with the advent of hippies, Valley Girls, MTV, hackers, yuppies, punkers, and rappers—and not always for the better.

The writer is like an architect who has designed a building. Grammar, usage, and spelling are the nails that hold the building together. Shoddy materials, like shoddy writing, mar the finished work. Throw the rusty nails out of your toolbox, and use the best material you can. Writing is not easy, though we are deceived when we read a fine book because it seems effortless—to those who haven't tried to do the same. I remember watching Dorothy Hamill skating her way to a gold medal in the Olympics: she made that look easy, too. But her triumph required years of practice and devotion, and many falls on the ice, before she became a champion.

The best way to learn to write is to read, read, and read, then write, write, and write. It may take years to learn how to Show-Don't-Tell, but one day you will begin to do it without thinking. Editors will always read manuscripts that are well crafted before those that are not, and this will increase your chance of getting published. But do not let concern over doing what is right get in the way of your creativity and originality: learn the rules, use the tools, until they are part of you. Then you can relax and forget them, because they'll be there when you need them for creating the best work you can.

PART II
And After

8 Making It Legal

GOOD NEWS! YOU'VE just heard from Annabelle Jones, the editor at Bench Press to whom you'd sent your novel, *Eating Dogfood Is No Fun*. She wants to buy it! She is offering you an advance of $1,500, against a straight royalty of 10 percent, and wants you to revise and deliver the manuscript in three months. She also tells you Bench Press plans to publish the book a year and a half from today. You're so delighted at the news and Annabelle's offer, your first impulse is to say, "Great! Send me the contract."

Even though you're secretly willing to pay Bench Press, stop and think for a moment. Assuming you have no agent, are you ready to negotiate the contract with Annabelle now? Or do you need time to collect your thoughts? If so, thank her for the news, and tell her you'll call her back with your decision. This is not the time, when you're excited and happy—and flustered—to commit yourself to a deal. Catch your breath. If possible, call up a few writer friends who've been published. Then, within a day or so, call Annabelle back.

Now that you've done some research, you've discovered that Annabelle's offer is at the low end of the scale for first or second books—the going rate is between $1,500 and $4,000. You have room for negotiation here. You may not get what you ask for, but asking doesn't hurt and may get you more than the original offer. So don't be shy. If Annabelle refuses to increase the advance, it's up to you whether to (a) accept it graciously, (b) withdraw the book, or (c) think of some ploys that might persuade her.

Many books have been written on the art of negotiating and on negotiating book contracts in particular. In all negotiations, each side must feel it's gained something for whatever it may have given up. Contracts contain many clauses that have nothing to do with the advance. Before you ever get a call from an editor, you should have familiarized yourself with those clauses for your own protection and to give yourself room to negotiate. The SCBW has a pamphlet, "Answers to Some Questions about Contracts," which is a helpful introduction to some of the legal questions, such as reversion of rights, you will be facing when you sell your work.

Annabelle also mentioned a royalty rate of 10 percent. A royalty is a percentage of the price for each copy sold, part of which is used to pay off the money the publisher advanced. As a consequence, you will receive no more cash until the advance is earned out. Annabelle probably based the advance on a conservative estimate of how many copies of *Eating Dogfood* would be sold in a year; it is her job to pay you as little as possible to minimize risk and maximize profit.

Assume the book will sell for $13.95; at a 10 percent royalty you will be credited $1.395 per copy. After 1,075 copies have been sold, you will be in the black, and, if sales continue, you will eventually receive royalty statements and checks, usually twice a year. Surely, you think, *Eating Dogfood* will sell more than 1,075 copies in the first year. Pick up your calculator.

In addition to advances, royalties, and delivery dates, territorial and subsidiary rights are also negotiable. For example, you might tell Annabelle that you want $2,500 for the book because you hope the book will sell at least two thousand copies the first year (at $13.95 this will equal $2,790) and will earn out the advance—with room to spare.

In addition, remind Annabelle that since you have no agent, you're selling world rights to Bench Press. Agents usually withhold foreign rights from publishers to sell themselves, and it will be advantageous to Bench Press to be able to sell *Eating Dogfood* all over the world and not just within a limited number of countries (usually the United States, the Philippines, Canada, and U.S. dependencies like the Virgin Islands and Guam.) It's likely that Annabelle will come up with a compromise figure after you've pointed this out.

Territorial rights are important, especially since after 1992 England is part of the European Community. That means if an American publisher sells English-language rights to a British publisher, it can sell the book in the EC countries, unless the U.S. publisher has laid claim to them first. Well before 1992 U.S. editors began buying world English-language rights from agents—and paying more—to ensure that American books will be sold in Europe by U.S. publishers, not British ones.

Then ask Annabelle how the advance will be paid. The usual way is for the publisher to pay half when the contract has been signed and the other half when the book has been delivered and the editor has declared it's "acceptable." Sometimes a publisher will want to hold back the second half of the advance until publication. Try not to let that happen, because it will mean a long wait until you see your money; in this case, at least eighteen months and possibly longer if publication is delayed. If Annabelle insists, try to get her to agree to a specific payment date instead, such as the first of the year. Sometimes publishers will split large advances into thirds: one third on signing, one third on acceptance of manuscript, and one third on publication, but this rarely happens with an advance under $10,000.

You can also ask Annabelle for an escalated royalty. For example, you might ask that the royalty increase to 12½ percent after ten thousand copies have been sold, then escalate again to 15 percent after twenty thousand copies have been sold. The probability of a first novel's selling over ten thousand hardcover copies is low, but if it does, then both you and Bench Press will be rewarded.

Contracts also specify royalty rates for sales other than the usual trade and library ones. These might include export sales, "special sales," certain book club sales, and so on. This is not the time to negotiate those; wait until you see the contract itself. Often these rates are part of the publisher's "boilerplate," and are not negotiable. The boilerplate is all the material printed in the contract as opposed to what is typed in. It's almost impossible for a new writer to change the boilerplate clauses, although agents can manage to "soften" or "dilute" them.

Territory affects the part of the contract referring to subsidiary rights, since the publisher can only sell rights it has purchased from the writer for specific territories. But "territory" is different from subsidiary rights. "Sub rights" usually include the following:

British publication, in English, including the EC
foreign-language translations
mass-market paperback

trade paperback

first serial (publication in magazines, etc., before the book is
    published)

second serial (publication in magazines, etc., after the book is
    published)

textbook

large print

anthologies

book club

performance (motion pictures, plays, TV, radio, etc.)

computer software

and "all other rights not specifically mentioned above"

The income from subsidiary rights sales is divided between the
publisher and the author, and the "splits" can vary. For example, is
Bench Press planning to publish *Eating Dogfood* in hardcover and
then in its own paperback line, and offering you an advance based
on a hard/soft deal? If so, your advance should be higher, and you
should negotiate a separate royalty schedule for the paperback now.
Or are they buying hardcover rights and hoping to sell the paperback rights to a mass-market house? What is the split?

Although you can ask for better terms, it's usually not worth
haggling over the subsidiary rights splits in the cases of first serial
and second serial rights. These rights can be lucrative in the world
of adult books, but the sums are negligible in juvenile publishing.
However, you should definitely *ask* for a larger share than 50–50 for
foreign rights, paperback, merchandise, and performance rights,
trying for 90–10 (you get the higher figure) and accepting less if
necessary; for example, 80–20, 75–25, 60–40. If the publisher will
not budge, don't be adamant, because there's no guarantee these
rights will ever be sold, and the argument may end up being aca-
demic. One author walked away from an otherwise good contract
for her first book because the publisher would not give in on the
50–50 paperback split; a year later she was still trying to sell the
book to another publisher.

You are also free to withhold certain rights, which means you
are free to attempt to sell them yourself. This can be important in
the case of illustrators who have created a character. On the other
hand, it's not easy to sell rights when you're a lone author, so it's
usually best to let the publisher have a go at it first.

Did Annabelle mention the option clause? Technically, this is not a true "option clause" but a right of first refusal. This means that you are obliged to send your next manuscript to Bench Press. It's not one to fret about. However, if you are already selling books to other publishers, it would be impossible for you to honor the option clause, and you should tell Annabelle so. She might then suggest wording such as "first refusal on a book with the same characters" or "for readers of the same age" or simply delete it altogether. It's in your interest as well as that of Bench Press to have more than one book from you on its list, so you should probably agree to this.

Your contract should contain a reversion of rights clause. If your book goes out of print, and you believe another publisher might want to reissue it, you must have the rights returned to you by the original publisher before you can publish the book elsewhere. Some publishers will not revert rights if any edition (for example, Danish large print) is in print anywhere, so read this clause carefully, and ask that the in-print provision refer only to English-language rights. After all, will the fact that your book is still in print in its Danish edition affect sales in North America?

How long it will take to receive the contract depends on the publishing house and the amount of bureaucracy entailed. These days, before an editor can get a contract for an author, she may have to fill out a form specifying the advance, royalty rate, number of book pages, quantity to be printed, cost of artwork, and so forth, and send it to the production department for an estimate of how much it will cost to manufacture the book. Then a business manager will take that figure and do a "profit-and-loss" analysis (the names of these steps differ, but the aim is the same: to find out whether it is financially feasible to publish the book).

If the numbers work out, the editor will then fill out another form, a contract request, and give it to the editorial director for approval. If all goes well, the editorial director will then ask the publisher or president of the firm to approve the request. Finally, a month or so later (depending on whether all the principals are available), the contract request will reach the contract department, where it will wait its turn to be typed. It then goes back to the editor for checking. Sometimes the typed contract circulates once again to the editorial director and publisher. Be warned: this cycle can take months, and much of it is beyond the control of your editor. Finally, you, the author, will get it, with a request to sign all the copies.

This long waiting period can be hard on the nerves, but try to relax and use the time to familiarize yourself with standard contract terms, through your reading and possibly by going over a sample contract with a knowledgeable friend. When your contract arrives, make the time to read it carefully, taking notes. It seems that nothing is as boring as a legal document, which is probably one reason why people pay lawyers such high fees. (Do lawyers make them boring for this reason?) As I was writing this I glanced over a contract I signed in 1976; it contained twenty-four clauses, most of them boilerplate. A more recent contract contained thirty-seven clauses, covering contingencies unheard of in 1976, such as computer software, and including items, such as libel insurance, deemed necessary because of recent lawsuits.

If you are well informed about negotiations because of your research and are dealing with a major, reputable publisher, it is rarely necessary to hire a lawyer to screen a contract for a first or second book, since so many of the terms are standard, with little leeway for improvement. In addition, few lawyers are experts in *publishing* law, a specialty in itself—let alone children's books as opposed to adult books—and often ask for terms that are unrealistic. Still, you may feel more comfortable having a lawyer's advice, as you would before signing any other contract. Laws would not exist were there no abuses.

Again, the art of negotiating lies in the ability to compromise. Still, if you are presented with a contract for a first or second book, remember, too, that the name of the game is Publication, and the first rule is Track Record. While you should not allow yourself to be cheated (and reputable publishers don't want to cheat you), you will be bargaining from strength the more successful your books are.

The ramifications of publishing law are endlessly varied. Some contracts contain a clause enjoining the writer not to write for any other publisher until the book under contract is finished. Obviously, if Bench Press has Mr. Best Seller under contract for one zillion dollars, it will not be in its interest for Mr. B.S. to write for another publisher while one third or half of one zillion dollars is accruing interest in his bank account and Bench Press is making loan payments at a high rate of interest.

Another issue under discussion is whether a writer has the right to keep an advance upon delivery of an acceptable manuscript that has fulfilled the terms of the contract but which the publisher has elected not to publish. There have been lawsuits over the definition of "acceptable," as well. These issues concern writers of adult books for the most part.

It's the rare writer who grasps all the fine points of negotiating a contract and who is able to press all his demands successfully. For the purposes of discussion, we've assumed that you have no agent. Although many well-known writers for children are without agents, they can be immensely useful.

For one thing, during the course of trying to sell *Eating Dogfood*, you would have been spared the form rejection letter. Your agent, who may have received more than one personal letter from editors, softened the blows when she told you the manuscript had been declined. She was sympathetic when you called the editors idiots. She also sent the manuscript out again without going into a depression. This was important, since you couldn't sell material buried in the closet. Because she is abreast of the market and knows the editors personally, it was she who thought Annabelle would like *Eating Dogfood*. Now, after an appropriate interval, she can call and remind Annabelle about the contract, which you would have found it impossible to do. But most important, she has negotiated the contract and will go over it carefully before you sign it. She is aware of potentially damaging clauses of which you have no inkling.

During a contract negotiation, the editor and author have a business relationship. This is another good reason to have an agent. Should there be any acrimony over the contract, let it be between agent and editor, not between author and editor.

Whether to have an agent is up to you. If you hate fine print with numbers embedded in it, you might prefer to have a specialist vet your contracts. On the other hand, it's part of the business of being a professional writer to know what you are signing. No one has a greater incentive than you when it comes to protecting your interests. And only you can decide whether paying 10 or 15 percent of a small advance and royalties is worth it. However, the time to choose an agent is not when you are offered a contract, but long before.

Still, now that you are faced with the Bench Press contract, you feel you should finally have an agent. It's much easier to get an agent to take you on once a contract is in the offing. However, *if you have already agreed to the terms* with Annabelle, your brand-new agent should not renegotiate them. This can result in serious damage to your career with Annabelle and Bench Press, who will resent such an "after-the-fact" negotiation and may even decide to cancel the offer. Also, unless you've already researched the field and know which agent you want, you may, in your haste, choose one who is not right for you.

Not too long ago, an author, Ms. X, and I had come to an agreement over the advance and royalties for her first novel, and a hard/soft contract was in process. Then one day the phone rang. An agent told me he was now representing Ms. X, and he demanded new terms. We agreed, but the agent was so demanding that my relationship with the author began to go sour.

For one thing, I had to retrieve the contract request from the editorial director and explain to him why the terms were being changed. Fortunately, the contract request had not yet reached the president's desk! She probably would have said forget the deal.

Then, before we published Ms. X's first book, the agent sent me a manuscript for a second novel, which needed work. But when I asked for extensive revisions, the agent advised Ms. X not to make them, and sold the book to another publisher, who published it in paperback only. As an editor, I felt betrayed, and the editorial director lost interest in Ms. X, since she was no longer exclusive with us.

By following that agent's advice, Ms. X, whom we had told had a good chance of becoming one of our star writers, lost a valuable opportunity. To make matters worse, the agent forced Ms. X to sign a two-book contract with him, so that Ms. X could not leave him until he had sold two books. By the way, the demands the agent made for the first book did not add up to enough money to cover his commission plus costs! Ms. X had picked him from a list in a writers' magazine, and he had had no experience in children's publishing.

A horror story like this should point up the fact that the choice of an agent is extremely important. They are not all equal. Some think money is more important than building a career, and will push writers to grind out books of inferior quality. An agent like this may be right for you, if fast money is your most important consideration. On the other hand, with a few exceptions, building a career takes time. One of your books may hit it big immediately, but usually a writer has produced ten or more titles before his name becomes a favorite with readers, librarians, and booksellers.

Whatever your personal goal may be, your agent should understand it and work with you, not against you, which is why, if you decide to have an agent, you should be represented *before* a contract is offered, or at least before you agree to *any* terms. And you should look for an agent who represents writers of children's books, which are handled differently from adult books.

An agent can perform another important service for you, which is to check your manuscript for possible instances of defamation, copyright violation, and other legal problems. Your editor will also be on the lookout for legal snags, especially if you have quoted material such as songs or poetry in your novel. But, as always, it is you, the author, who must be aware of possible legal pitfalls.

But *Eating Dogfood* is a novel, you say, a work of fiction. What can possibly give rise to legal action in a children's book? First off, you show Elvis eating canned dogfood in that memorable scene when Jennifer and Rodney find him. Are you sure canned dogfood is edible by human beings? There's always a chance, after reading your novel, that some child will eat dogfood and get sick. His parents might sue. A few letters to the major manufacturers will clarify this point. You might even decide to specify the brand of dogfood Elvis eats, if the manufacturer has told you it's safe for human consumption.

On the other hand you should be circumspect when calling products by their brand names. A negative statement about the product (" 'Poochy-Keen dogfood made me throw up,' said Elvis") may result in a lawsuit from the makers of Poochy-Keen, especially if the statement is questionable. Is it permissible to say something negative about a product if it's true? Probably, if you have proof, preferably from more than one source. But is it really necessary in the context of your novel?

Where did you get your story idea? Is it based on the divorce of your neighbors, Jane and Peter Nuñez? Millions of people get divorced, so there's nothing wrong in writing about a divorce. But how many of your story details come from the Nuñezes' divorce? Did their son run away? Be careful. Changing their names to Jean and Paul Perez is not sufficient to disguise them. You may be invading the privacy of your neighbors, and they may sue. If the Nuñez divorce made headlines in your community because their son ran away, you may be off the hook, since you are basing the novel on public knowledge, not private. However, if you are writing about people recognizable in your community, you may still be guilty of defamation because of some of your fictional details (e.g., "Mr. Perez was having an affair with his secretary"), which are not true but can be embarrassing to the Nuñezes. (Defamation in writing is called libel; in speech it's termed slander. Currently, because of the use of written material in a spoken medium like TV, the term "defamation" is being used more often.)

Perhaps you wished to pay tribute to Frank Bazyk, the counselor in your child's school, and you've given the counselor in *Eating Dogfood* the name Frank Bazyk. Jennifer calls him for help, but Mr. Bazyk says he can't do anything because he's going away on a business trip. That's a good plot device—an obstacle—but the real Frank Bazyk may not like your showing the fictional Frank Bazyk in this light. "It's false," he charges. "I'd never let a student down." "False light" may be considered defamatory, because your portrait of Frank Bazyk may tend to cause his colleagues and neighbors to have a low opinion of him. You certainly didn't mean any harm, but the real Frank Bazyk may decide to sue anyway.

The cases above may seem unlikely lawsuits, but who would have imagined a nurse would sue Ken Kesey for allegedly describing her in *One Flew over the Cuckoo's Nest*? She lost the case, but similar cases have been won recently. For example, an adult novel, published in hardcover, was never published in paperback, because the author's former wife alleged that the unfavorable portrait of the "former wife" in the novel was based on her, and she obtained an injunction pending settlement of the suit. The author insisted the former wife was entirely fictional; the former wife said, "No, she wasn't!" and cited *witnessed* details from their life together. In short, avoid basing your characters entirely on real people.

You may argue that writers have always relied on real events and people for fiction. But we are in litigious times, and today, if there were a real Madame Bovary, she might sue Flaubert unless he had completely disguised her character by changing her physical description, the place where she lived, and even, perhaps, her sex. The good news is that a real Anna Karenina cannot sue today's Tolstoy, because she is dead. However, even that's no guarantee, because courts *have* permitted families to sue on behalf of deceased family members when a reputation is at stake.

Go back and look at the warranty clause in your contract. You will agree to it (you have no choice), and one of the subclauses states that you "warrant," or guarantee, that the book contains no recipe, formula, or instruction that may harm the user. You've also guaranteed you have not invaded the privacy of a third person or stated anything libelous about him.

Some contracts also warrant that the book contains nothing obscene. Given the many differing interpretations of obscenity, you can ask that the obscenity clause be stricken out.

The situation is somewhat different for nonfiction. Public figures such as politicians, actors, and athletes have less of a claim to privacy because they are in the public eye and have been written about in newspapers, magazines, and books. Still, they are protected by law against false claims. When writing a biography about a living public figure, be especially wary of fictionalizing dialog— do not put false words into your subject's mouth. Since it is not always clear who is or is not a public figure—judges may disagree about someone like Frank Bazyk, the school counselor—it's best to consult with your editor.

If you are interviewing anyone for your book, you should have his consent to use the material, especially if the interview covers personal or potentially controversial information. The same rule holds true for photographs. A written or tape-recorded release may be required, but note that minors cannot give valid releases. Remember, too, that photographs taken on private property or of people in a private setting also usually require releases. If you are buying rights to photographs from a reputable, established source, the source has already obtained the releases—but check to make sure.

Never use a real telephone number or address in a book unless it's yours, and you're willing to accept the consequences. Robert Cormier used his own number in *I Am the Cheese* and has received many calls since the book was published, but that was his choice. A stranger would not appreciate your listing his number. If you need to use a telephone number, the telephone company suggests you use the prefix 555.

Is all this legal caution detrimental to the freedom of the press guaranteed under the First Amendment? Possibly, but under the Constitution the freedom of private persons is also protected. How do you balance the two? First, by using common sense; second, by asking Annabelle to send your manuscript to the Bench Press attorneys for vetting, if you have any doubt about what is permissible. Their advice may turn out to be wrong—no one can predict how judges will rule in an actual court case—but by acting on it, you are entitled to their protection should a lawsuit become a reality. Because of some noted defamation cases in the last decade, many publishers now carry liability insurance for claims over $50,000 alleging defamation, invasion of privacy, and trademark and copyright infringement. But do not count too much on this insurance: it affects only amounts over $50,000 or so; you may be liable for the rest.

Annabelle and the copy editors at Bench Press will keep an eye out for copyright violation, and you should, too. This usually involves material that requires written permission, such as songs, poems, and quotations from other sources. Sometimes the editorial staff will obtain permissions for you. Other times it will be your responsibility; your editor will help you by providing an appropriate form letter you can use.

First, you should understand which material is protected by copyright. Any written material copyrighted before 1978, when a new law went into effect, was protected by copyright for 28 years, with the right of renewal for another 28, for a total of a maximum of 56 years. The new law extends the renewal term to 47 years, for a total of 75 years. Therefore, *in general*, works published more than 75 years ago are in the "public domain"; that is, they are no longer protected by copyright *unless the author has been dead for fewer than fifty years*. The current law states that material will enjoy copyright protection for fifty years after the death of the author. For example, Lucy Maud Montgomery died in 1942. Even though *Anne of Green Gables* was published in 1908, it was not until 1992 that it entered the public domain.

The purpose of the copyright law is to protect artistic property and to guarantee that the owner of the copyright is reimbursed for its use. Any work *created* after December 31, 1977, is protected from the moment of creation; it need not be published! Therefore there is no need to register your work with the U.S. Copyright Office before publication, as long as you can prove it is your creation. Some writers safeguard their work by mailing it to themselves via certified mail, and leaving the envelope sealed. This is one way of proving when you wrote your novel. Another way is to have witnesses, such as family or friends, who have read your work soon after creation.

Since your novel will enjoy the benefits of the copyright laws, you should do all you can to honor the copyrights of others. The way to do this is to obtain permission to use copyrighted material in your book.

Expect to pay a fee for the use of copyrighted material. Fees vary, depending on the source. One famous songwriter demanded $100 for the use of just the five-word *title* of his song in a novel. As a rule of thumb consider the amount of material quoted in relation to the total work. For example, quoting 300 words from a book-length work, 150 words from a magazine article, and 50 words from a newspaper article is *generally* (not always) considered "fair use," and requires neither permission nor a fee. On the other hand, the use of a couple of lines from a short poem or song will probably require permission and a fee. If there's any doubt about whether to ask for permission, Annabelle will check with the contracts department.

Songs can be especially expensive. After one contemporary songwriter asked $1,500 for the use of a few lines from one of his songs, the author decided to invent her own lyrics. Check your contract: permission fees will be either deducted from your royalties or you may have to pay them *in advance of publication*. These can mount up, so be prudent in quoting copyrighted material.

If you're speedy enough, you might see the copyright lines on TV commercials. They are protected, too, as we found out when the hero recited a few in Betsy Byars's book, *The TV Kid*. The appropriate acknowledgments appear on the copyright page.

Sometimes a publisher may give an author a grant to cover permissions if the work in question is an anthology of poetry or short stories. Or the permission fees will be divided equally between author and publisher. Obviously, this is an item that must be negotiated in advance.

Be wary of unpublished material such as letters, journals, and manuscripts. You may own a letter from Mr. Famous, but you do not own the publication rights to it; Mr. Famous or his heirs own those.

You may also need permission to quote from your *own* published work. Therefore, if any part of your work has been published before, please tell your editor. You will note on some copyright pages, for example, that a certain book had first appeared in a magazine. Even when the material is copyrighted in the writer's name, his contract with the magazine may have given *it* the right to allow reprinting of his material.

The good news is that titles cannot be copyrighted. However, in practice, a title may have "meaning and value in the marketplace," and your use of it may present problems; don't call your novel about a tornado *Gone With the Wind*! Also, some titles have been registered as trademarks (Teenage Mutant Ninja Turtles, for one), and if you use them you may be violating trademark law. You may have a character in your book called Donald Duck (I once knew a boy with that name, believe it or not), but Walt Disney will not look with favor on seeing that name in a title. When Kevin Major wanted to use the title *Dear Bruce Springsteen*, he wrote to Springsteen for his permission. Think twice before using any licensed characters anywhere, including on T-shirts, which may end up depicted on book jackets.

If you are to obtain illustrations for your book, you may also be responsible for obtaining permission for their use and for paying any reproduction fees. In general, illustrations do not require permission or the payment of a fee if they were created by a government agency funded by U.S. taxpayers or if they first appeared in a book published more than seventy-five years ago. As with unpublished letters, don't assume that the owner of the illustrations has the reproduction rights to it. The New York Public Library, for example, has a fine picture collection, but you must apply to the copyright owners (photo agencies, magazines, etc.) for permission to use the wonderful illustrations you find there.

Even when text or art does not require permission, it is a courtesy to credit the source, which is usually done on the copyright page.

Someone once wrote me that she wanted to have a comedian as one of the characters in her novel. "Do I have to make up my own jokes?" she asked. "Should I use jokes from published collections (and get permission)? What about jokes I've heard?" Good questions. I'd often wondered myself about jokes. Where do they come from? I asked several people who know about such things, and they said the copyright of jokes is a thorny matter, with no hard and fast answers. For example, novelty is not a requirement for copyright, and ideas cannot be copyrighted. The experts offered these rules:

1. The longer the joke, the more concerned you should be about copyright; either forget the joke or get permission from the source. Shaggy-dog stories would fall into this category, for example.

2. If you use a short joke like a knock-knock or light-bulb one, change the wording if possible.

3. If the joke was printed, get permission.

4. If you heard the joke on the radio or TV, attribute it to the source.

If you are clear in your mind about the legal and financial details, signing a contract is a joyous occasion. Take each step as it comes, and get back to the typewriter! Remember, you've promised Annabelle she'd get the revised manuscript within three months. The name of the game is Publication, and you're on your way.

9 Bookmaking

A BULKY ENVELOPE arrives in the mail one day. The return address says Bench Press. You tear open the envelope and peek inside. Yes, it's your edited manuscript for *Eating Dogfood Is No Fun*, with a long letter from Annabelle Jones attached. You pull the papers out and glance at the letter. You're dying to know what she said, but part of you is afraid to read it. The word "wonderful" pops out at you. You relax a bit, and run your eye farther down the page. Another word pops out: "unconvincing." You shove the papers back into the envelope. Wasn't this the day you were going to clean behind the stove?

Some writers can't wait to see what the editor has to say about their manuscripts. Others want to shove the whole thing into a drawer and go to South America for a few years. But sooner or later, all writers must sit down with their edited manuscripts and the editorial letters and come to terms with them.

We all love praise, and Annabelle's first paragraph is full of it. She's said the manuscript is "moving" and "profound." That's true, and how perceptive of her to recognize the many fine qualities in *Eating Dogfood*. Now on to paragraph two, which begins with the word "however" and goes on to point out all the flaws in the manuscript. Paragraph after paragraph, that woman does nothing but criticize! Well, you realize, some of the points are well taken and easy to fix; others are not. Her remark about the unsatisfactory ending is just plain stupid! You begin to sweat. Can you deal with this? Ah, at the end of the letter she's back to saying the manuscript is splendid. "An important book," she calls it. Maybe you *can* work on the manuscript a little more. Or should you get down to cleaning behind the stove first?

Whatever your next step is, you know that you will reread Annabelle's letter—many times. You will also go through your novel page by page to see her remarks. Some you will agree with immediately; others you will take issue with. Maybe you'll let a few days go by to give her suggestions time to sink in. After that you'll get down to tackling the revisions, trying to keep in mind that Annabelle has offered *suggestions*, not commands, and that you are the writer and must trust yourself.

When it comes to publishing a book, the most rewarding author–editor relationship should be a partnership, where both parties work toward the same end: the best book possible. Annabelle has spent many hours thinking about your work and making notes for improvement. Her suggestions are based on years of education and experience, including voracious reading throughout her life. She may not be right about everything, but there is no one else you can trust to be as impartial and honest about your writing. Your spouse and friends are either "too busy" or too adoring; other writers are often jealous; reviewers may have private axes to grind. Annabelle sits between your virgin manuscript and the public. She is the first real reader *Eating Dogfood* has been exposed to, and like a kindly parent, she is the first to say "your slip is showing." But don't forget: she liked your book enough to buy it!

The manuscript for my first novel, *The High Voyage*, came back to me looking as if a sooty chicken had wandered over every page. I resented each change my editor, Cary Ryan, had tactfully suggested, because I'd worked hard on my book and didn't want to believe that I wasn't perfect. On another book, the editor, Jill Hartman, kept insisting an explanation was unclear, even after I'd rewritten it three times: "If I can't understand it, how can you expect a child to?" she asked.

An editor seldom gets credit for her work, which includes preventing your murky or ungrammatical passages from going out into the world. Still, no matter how much the editor may have helped, the book belongs to the writer. I've rarely seen a book criticized for being poorly edited, often for being poorly written.

Therefore, at some point your judgment has to supersede Annabelle's. You've thoughtfully weighed all her suggestions and done as much as you thought necessary. But the ending still worries you, because Annabelle has said it's too abrupt. You think it's fine, and that she's missed the irony. You don't want to change it. What should you do?

Go back to the beginning. Reread Annabelle's letter. You're satisfied that the additional work you've done on Jennifer's character has made her actions convincing. You've added more details about Elvis to strengthen his motivation. And you must admit Annabelle had a great idea about Rodney's flat tire. This new scene of yours, where Jennifer and Rodney fix the tire, shows them interacting in such a way that it further develops their characters and deepens their relationship. It also intensifies the conflict between Jennifer and Rodney—their relationship was a bit too smooth to be interesting.

Now go through the manuscript again. Annabelle has carefully bracketed all the passages she thought should be cut and explained why. You admit to yourself that she was right most of the time; the manuscript has become more "show" than "tell." You still blush at how many times you had Jennifer blush and Rodney nod! Annabelle has marked each instance to draw your attention to these blind spots. She has not rewritten long passages, but here and there she's improved on transitions and wording, and you let her changes stand. It *is* a better book, and you're grateful.

Taking all this into account, could she also be right about the ending? You've been so immersed in *Eating Dogfood Is No Fun* that you can't be sure any longer. Don't despair. Leave the ending alone and send the manuscript back to Annabelle; you'll have another chance to see it, after copyediting and before it is set in type. The time has come to let go for now.

Back at Bench Press, Annabelle has been busy, too. She's preparing for a sales conference in Florida, reading and editing other manuscripts, and seeing a number of books through production. She's also avoiding phone calls from writers and agents, who are looking for word about manuscripts and contracts. With a hundred or so unread manuscripts in her office, Annabelle plans to get to everything when she can, but production deadlines take priority. She also hates to answer telephone calls about contracts that are slowly making their ways through the Bench Press bureaucracy. She sighs. So little of her time, perhaps 15 to 20 percent, is spent reading and editing manuscripts, and she longs for the old days when publishing was better staffed. Then the revised manuscript for *Eating Dogfood* arrives on her desk.

Believe it or not, she's thrilled to get it. This is one of the highlights of her job, seeing the result of your work together. She took on *Eating Dogfood Is No Fun* not only because she liked the book but because she hopes you will develop into a productive and honored writer. Unfortunately, she can't spare the time now to read the manuscript. The sales conference looms ahead, and she has a great deal to do. She stuffs the manuscript into her briefcase; she'll read it at home.

In spite of her good intentions, Annabelle doesn't get around to reading your manuscript until a few months later. You haven't heard a word from her, and you're concerned. Don't be.

During this time Annabelle and the art director have discussed possible illustrators for your book, and they have commissioned Melissa Hoffman, who will do six black-and-white drawings for the book.

If the silence weighs heavily on you, call her or drop her a note asking whether she's received the manuscript. That will remind her it's with her, and she must get around to reading it soon. Not only are you waiting for word—perhaps the manuscript was lost in the mail—you are also waiting for the second part of the advance due on acceptance.

Finally Annabelle reads the revised manuscript and is satisfied. She telephones you, apologizing for her silence, and reassures you that all is well—except for the ending, which she thinks is still too abrupt. "I'm transmitting the manuscript anyway," she tells you. "Take another look at the ending when you see the copyedited manuscript about three weeks from now."

If Annabelle doesn't mention the second payment, remind her. The contract signing was so long ago, she's likely to have forgotten about the payment. But you want to know: is the manuscript acceptable? (Some editors do not consider a manuscript acceptable until the writer has made *all* the revisions; others will give the writer the benefit of the doubt and declare the manuscript acceptable even though more work is needed.) Luckily, Annabelle says, "I'm so sorry. I forgot. Don't worry, I'm requesting your check, and you should get it shortly. I'll also send you copies of Melissa's sketches when they come in." This is good news, and you go out to celebrate.

Meanwhile Annabelle or her assistant fills out yet more forms and gets ready to transmit your manuscript to production. She lists on a transmittal form all the material she is submitting to production and any she may be waiting for, such as an index or dedication. It's not just the text of your book that goes into production. A book has many parts, and she has to keep track of them all. Annabelle checks the material that goes at the front of every book (including the one you are now reading), known as the "front matter."

The first page of a book is usually the half title. The "half title" is just that: the title of the book—no subtitle, no author, no publisher. This page had its origins in the days when books were printed but sold without bindings; the buyer would have them bound elsewhere. The bookseller would stack the unbound books in his shop and identify them by the half title, which also served to protect the inside of the book from being damaged or soiled.

Page 2 is usually a blank or it may be an "ad card" (a list of your other books in chronological order) or it may contain an illustration or map and earn the name "frontispiece."

Facing the second page is page 3, the title page, which carries, at the least, the *official* title (and subtitle, if there is one) of your book, your name, the name of the illustrator, and the name and location of the publisher. Sometimes it carries the copyright notice, if space is tight.

Usually, however, the copyright is on a separate page, the "verso" of the title page, or page 4. In addition to the copyright notice and a statement "reserving all rights," the copyright page carries the full address of the publisher, a line indicating the edition, and the Library of Congress Cataloging in Publication (CIP) notice. Annabelle is responsible for obtaining the official copyright notice from the contracts department, which makes it conform to the publisher's style and to the contract, which carries *your* authorization to copyright the work and the name in which you wish the copyright to be registered. She requests the CIP from the Library of Congress itself. (The Library of Congress is proficient at ferreting out the birth year of authors—for identification purposes—and usually inserts it on the CIP; it's all right to ask that it be deleted in your book, which some publishers do as a matter of course.)

Another important piece of information on the copyright page is the International Standard Book Number (ISBN), which is the order number. The first digit is usually a zero, which stands for

"English language"; the next three indicate the publisher's code number; the next group of five is the number of your book, and the last is used for internal verification. In some ways the title and copyright pages are the most important pages of your book! Permission acknowledgments also appear on the copyright page if there's enough room.

It's long been the custom for writers to dedicate their work to someone. If you haven't included a dedication, someone may remind you, but don't count on it; it's your responsibility. The dedication usually appears on the first right-hand page after the copyright notice and is worded simply, "For X" or "To X". Every now and then a writer gets carried away and wants to dedicate his book to dozens of people. It's more professional to keep the dedication brief, because it's not meant to be a blanket "thank you" but a sincere wish to remember a particular person.

Sometimes it's appropriate to thank people for helping you with your book; this information should go on a separate acknowledgments page. This is usually unnecessary for a work of fiction unless someone has given you vital technical help. For works of nonfiction, an acknowledgments page is a necessary courtesy.

If your book has chapter titles (which is up to you), then a table of contents (simply headed "Contents") is needed. Type that up, along with the dedication, when you send in the manuscript.

Sometimes a writer will begin his book with a quotation from a poem or such. Known as the "epigraph," this also goes on a right-hand page after the dedication, if space permits.

A second half title or a part title may appear before the text proper begins. Part titles are necessary when a book is broken into parts, for instance, "Part One: Before the Divorce." The second half title is inserted at the discretion of the book designer.

In a nonfiction book, you may have to supply other front matter, such as a preface, foreword, author's note, or introduction. Nothing that appears before the table of contents should be listed in it (because it's not necessary), and this includes the preface, which is a short note, usually by the author.

A foreword is also short, but it is written by someone other than the author. An introduction is more extensive and may be written either by you or by someone else. If this material is not essential to the understanding of your text, it should appear as a preface, author's note, or foreword before the table of contents. For example, if you thanked your typist in an author's note, that is not essential to the understanding of your book. On the other hand, if you have important background to your text that must be understood, it is an introduction and part of the book itself, which qualifies it to appear after and in the table of contents.

You'll often see in old novels and new nonfiction a list of illustrations (headed "Illustrations"). This is considered old-fashioned for modern novels, but on occasion you or the editor may think it's necessary.

You may have been puzzled at seeing the numeral 3 on the first page of a novel or nonfiction work. That's because the front matter is usually numbered with small roman numerals, and they often aren't printed. If there's a part title, the two pages before the first text page are pages arabic 1 and arabic 2, because a part title is considered part of the text. In some books, the counting begins with arabic numerals in the front matter, so that the first page of text might carry a page number, or folio, reading 7 or 9. Most picture books have no folios because they interfere with the esthetics of the art and text. (This practice drives teachers and pupils up the wall, because they have to count the pages by hand.)

These details may seem like much ado about nothing, but bookmakers are proud of their long and venerable tradition, exemplified in how much attention is paid to the "little things." Also, in the world of publishing, all editors, designers, production people, compositors, printers, and binders speak the same language; it's helpful when a writer knows the jargon too.

If there is front matter, can back matter exist, too? Indeed it does. Again, this applies primarily to nonfiction, and the contents might list the following as part of the back matter: appendix, glossary, source notes, bibliography, and index. These sections should appear in this order, with index always last because it is not prepared until a late stage of the book.

Many publishers like to supply a short biography ("bio") of the author and illustrator at the end of the book. This is not officially part of the book because the writer didn't write it as part of the book. As a consequence, the page is not numbered, and the bio can be revised or deleted from future editions if necessary.

In the "good old days," publishers often put advertisements of their other titles ("house ads") on surplus pages ("blanks") at the backs of books. Today, however, hardcover publishers frown on this practice, but you will still see house ads at the backs of paperbacks. You might want to check your contract to see whether you've given permission to the publisher to insert *other than house ads* in your book; some paperback publishers sell space in books to outsiders, such as book clubs. I don't mind house ads at the back of a paperback, but an insert in the middle infuriates me. Books are almost our only refuge from commercial intrusions, and a writer can protect them by refusing to grant permission to carry advertising, except for house ads. It may seem hypocritical not to permit outside ads while approving of house ads, but a house ad may one day advertise your book at the back of someone else's; also the practice is so established that no one thinks twice about it any longer.

Speaking of advertising, Annabelle has also been thinking of the jacket for your book and has probably discussed it by now with the art director, who is responsible for finding an artist. Most writers are not aware that the dust jacket (hardcovers) or cover (paperbacks) is not their property but the publisher's. The publisher can put whatever it likes on the jacket or cover, because a jacket not only protects the book but also advertises it, enticing the reader to pick it up. Publishers love to have reviewers reprint the flap copy, because it's more glowing than any review will probably be. And even though the jacket art may be copyrighted in the artist's name, publishers also love it when the art appears in print, accompanying a review, as long as the author and title of the book are clear.

Meanwhile, Annabelle is still working on the transmittal form. Procedures vary somewhat at different houses, but Bench Press asks for the following information (in addition to the front matter, title, author, and so forth): The editor estimates how many pages the book will run, specifies the "trim" (the size of the page), the kind of binding, end sheets, quantity to be printed and bound, publication date, and type of art (if any). She will also give a brief description of the novel and suggest the sort of "look" the book should have: antique, traditional, contemporary, avant-garde, humorous, literary, and so on. And she will give instructions to the copy editor such as "no rewriting, please," or, in the case of a book from another English-speaking country, "Americanize spelling and query unusual words." Annabelle also writes a brief biographical note about you headed "About the Author" and tucks it at the back of the manuscript.

Finally, all the pieces are together, and Annabelle passes the manuscript on to the managing editor, who will check it to be sure the transmittal memo is in order. Annabelle has included extra copies of the manuscript. It's at this point that Bench Press considers the book to be an official entry on the next list, and the managing editor sends copies of the manuscript to the art, marketing, sales, subsidiary rights director, and anyone else in house who needs to read the book early.

The managing editor then sends the original manuscript and transmittal to the copyediting department. The copyediting department at Bench Press is small, so much of the work is sent out to freelancers. *Eating Dogfood* goes to crack copy editor Hilda Cross, who is a full-time copy editor at another house, but needs to supplement her income by doing extra work at home. She has a small but powerful library of reference books on her desk, and she refers to them often while working on your manuscript. Hilda keeps an alphabetical list of proper names and unusual spellings on a separate piece of paper called a style sheet. Any deviations from house style are also listed on the style sheet, which will later go to the proofreader for his reference.

Another of Hilda's jobs is to mistrust every objective fact in your book and check it. For example, you said azaleas were blooming in front of Jennifer's house, "their pink blossoms blending into the autumn foliage." Hilda knows azaleas are a spring flower, but she might look for a late-blooming variety in one of her reference books or even call a botanist. Or she might simply suggest you use another flower, since azaleas indicate spring to most people. In spite of Hilda's thoroughness, you cannot rely on the copy editor to check *all* your facts. She will spot-check a nonfiction manuscript, but cannot be expected to go to a university library and verify the page numbers in your source notes. If, during the spot checking, she finds an excess of errors, the entire manuscript may go back to you for further correcting.

Hilda will rewrite ungrammatical passages, correct your typographical errors and misspellings, and punctuate the book, following "house style." Each publisher has a list of rules it follows, and Hilda will conform to them. For example, some houses prefer the serial comma and others don't use it. What is a serial comma? It is the comma before "and" or "or" in a series of items: "bread, butter, and jam." Hilda's objective is to make your manuscript consistent so that "backyard" is not one word in one place and two in another and hyphenated on the jacket flap! She's an expert on the use of capital letters, hyphens, and apostrophes with possessives. She knows that adverbs ending in "-ly" are never linked to adjectives or nouns with hyphens. She's spelled out all abbreviations (e.g., "O.K." becomes "okay") and numbers used in dialog, which looks strange to you, but which is done because these are being *said* by a character.

You will also see Hilda's liberal use of proofreaders' marks: for example, she'll indicate a period by using a dot inside a circle, and will put circles around words or figures that should be spelled out. Nearly all dictionaries carry proofreaders' marks, and it's a good idea for writers to learn them—it's a shorthand publishers and printers use that not only saves us from long-winded explanations but also communicates our messages with precision.

Hilda will also indicate which material is to be treated differently, such as letters, verse, quotations (extracts), and she will flag the different levels of chapter headings (especially in nonfiction books) for the designer.

Sometimes Hilda will write "WIT" in the margin, meaning her source is *Words Into Type* or "Web 9," meaning the *Merriam-Webster Dictionary*, 9th edition. Hilda will also write queries and suggested changes on tags attached to the edges of the pages.

When you go over the manuscript, you can answer her queries directly on these tags or on the manuscript itself, in pencil, not ink. But don't tear off the tags, please; Annabelle needs to see them so that she will know what you and Hilda have done. Annabelle likes to go over the copyedited manuscript before she sends it to an author, because she can answer many of the questions herself, and, indeed, Hilda has addressed some to her. Annabelle will also go over the manuscript again when you return it.

Hilda's done her work in two weeks, and you have another two weeks to do your part. Here's your chance to rewrite the ending, if you've decided to do so. You can also make other small changes and, if necessary, rewrite whole sections, working directly on the manuscript. If your bio contains errors, correct them now. This is the same bio that will appear on the jacket. There's no need to retype pages with a few corrections. But when it begins to look like a drunken smorgasbord, it's safest to retype the entire page. Indicate at the top that it is a revision, and include the old or "foul" page when you return the manuscript.

One of the ironies of word processing is that writers feel compelled to submit "clean copy," and it seems easier to reprint the entire manuscript than to reprint a few pages here and there, which causes the page numbers to change. If you do reprint, be sure to include the old manuscript so that the editor can see where you've made the revisions. But if you're only changing words and sentences here and there, don't reprint; the compositor can follow slightly corrected copy and pages marked 132A and 132B with no difficulty. In the event you are asked to do a third revision (or fourth), it's best not to reprint. The margins of manuscripts contain the history of the editing, and if they are clean, future scholars will never know how you and your editor differed over whether to rewrite the ending of your novel.

The book is now on a schedule, and all deadlines must be met. If you were planning to use your advance for a two-week vacation in Mexico, wait until you've returned the copyedited manuscript. You'll have five to seven weeks before you see the next stage of production: galley proofs.

Eating Dogfood Is No Fun is now ready for the compositor—almost. While you were going over Hilda's remarks, a book designer was studying a copy of the manuscript, and doing a character count. Did you know that the average children's novel of between 160 and 192 pages may contain over a quarter of a million characters? In this sense a "character" is each letter, numeral, space, or punctuation mark in the manuscript. Of course, if you've worked with a word processor, you can get that count from your machine. If not, it has to be done by hand. Word counts usually are not necessary, but designers will be grateful if you supply character counts.

Once she has the character count, the designer chooses an appropriate typeface in a size that will fill the number of pages Annabelle has asked for. She may have the compositor set sample layouts using that face. Annabelle studies the layouts, and decides the book looks too crowded. She and the designer discuss the possibility of adding more pages to the book or of using a smaller type or less "leading" (the spaces between the lines). Annabelle usually approves the designer's choice of type, but she keeps an eye on the appropriateness of the page layout for the age level of the intended reader. The younger the reader, for example, the larger the type and the fewer lines of type per page. When Annabelle is satisfied with the layouts, the designer marks up the copyedited, final manuscript with the specifications. These include such items as the amount of space between the top of the page and the first line of each chapter ("sinkage"), where the folios will be placed, the style of the running heads (or feet) on each page, and much more. (Running heads usually appear at the top of each page, with the author's name on the left page and the title of the book on the right; when they are at the bottoms of pages, they are called "running feet.")

From design the manuscript goes to the production department. These are the people who select the printer and purchase the paper for your book. They are also the ones who gave Annabelle a cost estimate when she signed up your book. An enormous amount of material flows through their department as they send manuscripts and all stages of proofs back and forth between compositors, printers, separators, binders, and the editorial and design staff. And, when it's time for your book to go into a new printing, they will handle that too, as well as take care of special orders for book clubs and the like.

Off the manuscript goes at last to the compositor, and in about three weeks he'll return galley proofs. True "galleys" no longer exist, since that term referred to the days of "hot" lead linotype; compositors today can set type right into pages using computers. But traditionalists still call the first proofs galleys, while others call them first pass. Whatever the name, this is *the last time you will be able to revise your work.*

Some writers list all the changes, including PEs, or printer's errors, on separate pieces of paper; this is tedious, unwieldy, and unnecessary, because all of us are used to checking the margins of the galleys swiftly for corrections, and this is the safest place to make them; pieces of paper can get lost. In addition, changes written in the body of the text instead of in the margins will likely not be caught by all the people who will be working with your galleys. Here's where your knowledge of proofreaders' marks will come in handy!

Seeing your work in type gives it a permanence typewriting or handwriting cannot; it automatically looks more authoritative. Still, you may want to rewrite material for reasons of accuracy or felicity. Be cautious: a galley is not a blank check allowing you to rewrite at whim. According to your contract with Bench Press, you are allowed 10 percent of the "cost of composition" for making "author alterations," or AAs. Of course, you don't know the cost of composition! But for a novel assume about $2,000, which means you can make about $200 worth of changes for free. But keep in mind that this refers to two hundred *lines*, not two hundred words, and each line costs roughly two dollars to reset. If you take a word out of the first line of a paragraph, for example, the whole paragraph may need to be reset, resulting in perhaps a dozen line changes, which will cost about $25.00. AAs mount up quickly, and if you exceed your allowance, you will see this amount deducted from your royalties later on.

During the two weeks when you are checking the galleys, a professional proofreader is reading the "master set" against the original, copyedited manuscript. He may find some factual errors the copy editor, the editor, and you missed, and will correct them, along with catching PEs and style errors. He may come across a matter that only you can handle, and he'll flag that for Annabelle, who will call you to discuss it.

After you've returned your galleys, Annabelle or someone in the copyediting department will transfer your changes to the master set, which will then go back to the compositor for correcting.

Although this marks the end of your work on the text (so that you can head for a longer vacation in Mexico), the publisher's staff has a great deal more to do, including arranging for the right jacket for your novel.

By now Melissa's sketches for the jacket and interior of the book have come in. Annabelle has discussed them with her department head and the art director, and has shown the jacket sketch to the marketing and sales directors. Her assistant has checked the sketches against the manuscript to be sure all the details are correct. For example, on the jacket Jennifer has medium-length curly brown hair and wears glasses, which she is holding in her hand.

Annabelle is so thrilled with the sketches that she mails you copies. Not all editors do this, so don't be disappointed if you don't see the artwork. The package arrives just as you're leaving for the airport; you open it in the taxi. The sketch looks wonderful, showing the new scene with Jennifer and Rodney fixing the flat tire. Then you groan: the bicycle is wrong. You telephone Annabelle from the airport, and tell her, "Rodney has a trail bike; it's not a ten-speed. And why isn't Jennifer wearing her glasses?" Annabelle groans.

Illustrators usually use live models for their work, and if you are correct about that trail bike, Melissa will have to find one for Rodney and pose the model with it to be sure the leg is in proper relation to the pedals and the hands to the handlebars. Also, she'll have to get the model she used for Jennifer to pose with glasses on and do something else with her hands. Melissa will charge extra for these changes because she was not told what kind of bicycle to draw, and the art director asked her *not* to show Jennifer wearing glasses. The change that seems so minor to you is not as far as the artist is concerned, and many writers have difficulty understanding this fact. It's not that your editor doesn't want to please you, it's that changes are expensive to make and delay the production schedule. It's often much easier to change a few lines of type than the shape of a bicycle or the light and shadows on a face with glasses.

As you watch the clock in the airport, Annabelle frantically checks the manuscript. She finds no mention of the kind of bicycle Rodney owns, and tells you that the jacket sketch cannot be changed. "But it's important!" Annabelle doesn't budge, even though she'd like to please you. Often a writer is sure her mental picture of a scene was conveyed in the text; just as often, it was not. A writer once told me the girl in his book had black hair (the artist had made her a blonde). "But you never told us the color of her hair," I said. "Her mother had gypsy blood," he replied, "and I said that on page 37." I groaned and conceded the point; the artist made the change.

Many writers are unhappy with their jackets because they don't match the writers' images of scenes and characters. But you should remember that the artist brings his personal view to his work just as you bring yours. He's not hired to do an exact rendering of a scene but to do an esthetic interpretation that will also help sell the book. This holds true for the glasses, which Jennifer is holding, because she looks more attractive that way. "That's sexist," you say. Annabelle agrees with you, but she says, "Marketing insists, no glasses!"

As I said earlier, the jacket is the property of the publisher, who uses it almost like an ad to entice readers, especially those of junior-high age. Writers should insist that technical details be correct, as Todd Strasser did for his book *Beyond the Reef*, about treasure diving. He asked the artist to make a number of changes to be true to diving, which Strasser had researched. For example, the artist showed lumpy cloth bags being brought up from the sea. "Treasure divers use net bags," Strasser told me, "and the text specifies that the gold coins show through the netting." Nothing annoys a reader so much as inaccuracy in illustration, and editors are aware of that. If changes are necessary for objective editorial reasons they will be made.

But art and marketing directors and editors will argue over what they call subjective responses, such as the choice of colors or whether a girl in glasses will attract or repel readers. I haven't liked every jacket on books I've edited, but there comes a point when, unless there's an overwhelming reason to change or kill them, jackets must stand as painted.

Annabelle reassures you, however, that there's time to check the interior sketches, since they're not needed for production until later. Meanwhile, Melissa will finish the jacket painting. But you must get your comments to Annabelle about the interior art immediately on your return from Mexico, because Bench Press wants the final art in time to make BOMs, or bound galleys.

Once you've gone over the copyedited manuscript, read galleys, seen the jacket art, and checked the illustrations for the interior of the book, there's not much left for you to do as far as book production is concerned. It will be another six to nine months before you see the book itself, in all its glory. You should be well on your way in the writing of your next one, and thinking of ways to promote *Eating Dogfood*, but we'll get into that in the next chapter.

Meanwhile, Annabelle is still involved with your book. Over the next months she will be checking Melissa's artwork and three more stages of proof: second pass (or page proof), repros (reproduction proof), and blues, none of which you will see. She's also been checking the jacket in its various stages. Jackets and text for novels are printed at different places, and each one has its own schedule. At Bench Press, they want to be sure to have BOMs and jacket proofs for the sales conference, and the deadlines are tight.

Melissa's final art for the interior arrives, and Annabelle sends you copies. You can ask for corrections if the art still does not conform to the text, but sometimes it's easier to change the text, and Annabelle may ask you to do so. The copy editor has also checked the art against the galleys to be sure the details are correct. The final jacket is also in, and the designer has done a jacket mechanical (type and photostat of art pasted down and accurately measured for the printer). Now that the designer's choice of typeface for the jacket has been approved, she can set the display type for your book. "Display" is the large, ornamental type used for the title page and chapter headings. The designer chooses a face that will look well on the jacket and that will convey the spirit of the text. Sometimes a designer will use a stock ornament or even draw a small picture to go on chapter openings to dress up the inside of the book.

"God is in the details," said the architect Mies van der Rohe. Designers feel the same way, and when blues come in, with art and text stripped into place, designers check them to be sure everything is in place; this is the first time anyone sees what the book will actually look like when it is printed. A copy editor also checks the blues, not only for typos but to see that all the pages are there and in the right order. And Annabelle, too, looks over everything for the last time. Any corrections made at this stage are expensive, so everyone prays none will be necessary.

The book goes off to the printer, and finally to a binder, where it will also be jacketed. The first copies of the book arrive at Bench Press, and production checks them to be sure all is in order. Annabelle holds the book in her hands, opens it, and sniffs it. "Don't new books smell wonderful?" she asks.

At last, nine months or so after you sent back the copyedited manuscript, you get a package in the mail. You tear it open: it's *Eating Dogfood Is No Fun*, the first copy, hot off the press, as Annabelle tells you in her note. "Your contractual copies are on the way from the warehouse," she says, "but I knew you'd want to see this one first."

Your dream has come true. You are a published writer, and in your hands is the proof: a book with your name on it. Such a small thing, only a few ounces, yet it carries the labor and love of many people whom you'll never meet. It's like a newborn baby, and you wonder, as you hold it, what will happen when it goes out into the world. But that's another chapter.

10 Your Career Is Your Business

ONG BEFORE YOU held the finished copy of your novel, you and your editor were thinking of ways to publicize and sell it. Although *Eating Dogfood Is No Fun* is well written and tells a good story, it was the title that first caught Annabelle Jones's attention. She thought it would catch young readers' eyes as well. (Sometimes it seems that the right title for a book is more important than what is inside, but that's not true.) Annabelle also liked the setting—a resort town—the characters, and the name Elvis, which was a subtle clue to the character of the mother as well as being trendy. *Eating Dogfood* was not "another divorce book"; it had humor, romance, and showed the importance of communication within a family. Annabelle knew right away that she had a handle to use when presenting it to the sales reps. With the right jacket, the book was on its way to standing out from the thousands of other titles to be published that season.

Imagine yourself walking into a bookstore or library, looking for a book to read. If no one is around to help you—and there often isn't—how will you choose a book? Isn't it true that a jacket or title or an author's name will beckon to you? "Author recognition" is probably the most important influence on book buyers—readers are inclined to choose books by authors whom they know. If you don't have a famous name, you must have an appealing title and jacket to help you beckon to the reader. Annabelle knows that. What else can your editor do for you?

Consider that Annabelle has eight books on her list, and another twenty or so are coming from the other editors at Bench Press. Altogether there are nine novels for the same age group as

Eating Dogfood. One is by a Newbery Award–winner, three others are by well-established writers, and three are by people who've only published a few books each. *Eating Dogfood* and one other are first novels. And this is just one list. What about the thousand or so books coming from other publishers? Does an unknown writer have a chance, you ask?

Yes, because the systems established over the past years work well. What are they?

First, there's the biographical questionnaire, which Annabelle sent you months before. This gave you a chance to list influential people or associations you believe would be interested in a novel on the subject of divorce. You've also provided the names of local bookstore managers or owners, librarians, school officials, and—most important—the book reviewers on your local newspapers. You've racked your brains to think of other local people who might want to buy a copy of the book. Since it's about divorce, you've supplied the names of local clergymen, doctors, and counselors who work with young people. The more names and affiliations you can think of the better. Few people keep up with children's books, and some of those you've listed might be delighted to know that a book about divorce exists for kids! Bench Press will go over your list and decide who will receive review copies. Not so long ago, Bench Press would also send a press release about the book along with it; but the staff is too small to do that now.

When Annabelle wrote your bio, she made a point of listing schools you've attended, places you've lived, and where you live now. How much she included depended on space, of course. Being a "local author" doesn't mean much in a big city, but in small towns and suburbia, it can mean a great deal. Annabelle was sure to include your hometown in the catalog and on the jacket.

Annabelle's catalog copy is designed to make prospective purchasers eager to own your book. It's not only a summary of the story; it tells librarians and bookstore buyers that the book is special, and they must have it. The same is true of the copy that will appear on the flap of the book jacket.

By the time sales conference has come along, Annabelle has also drawn up a "tip sheet," which editors do for every book on the list. The tip sheet, which goes to each sales rep, provides the numbers (price, ISBN, age and grade levels, etc.) and a brief summary of the plot and information about the author. Annabelle also writes the "selling points," such as, in the case of *Eating Dogfood*, the statistics on divorce, special attributes of the book, and so on. If it's relevant, she'll also list the competition, and explain how your book is better than or different from the rest of the field.

About four months before publication date, Bench Press holds a sales conference (there are three a year, one for each publishing "season"; some publishers have only two). As a senior editor Annabelle attends the conference, though the other editors do not; she and the department head will present all the books. In a room full of sales reps and other Bench Press staff members, she talks about your book with great enthusiasm. The reps make notes on their tip sheets as she speaks, keeping one eye on a slide of the jacket, which is projected on a big screen in front of the audience. This is probably the first time the reps have heard of your book. A color photograph of the jacket and a bound galley of the book are in their sales kits so that they may read the book before going out to see their customers. If you have written a picture book, the reps will receive proofs of the book to show prospective buyers.

Annabelle is realistic: she knows that juvenile hardcover first novels are rarely placed in standard bookstores, but she hopes that a rep here and there will try to "sell in" this book, especially in the author's hometown and in children's-only bookstores. According to one survey, school libraries, public libraries, and bookstores each buy about one third of all middle-grade and YA fiction titles, with school and public libraries together making up over half the market. She also knows that the reps who deal with the school and library jobbers like Baker and Taylor are paying close attention, because the institutional wholesalers are the best customers for a book like yours. By and large the reps are most interested in Bench Press's adult books, though a few love children's books and will pay special attention to the juvenile list, especially to the picture books—over 40 percent of some books go to the bookstores.

A rep has only a short time to present a long list of books to each bookstore buyer, and he has to present them with an eye to what that buyer is most interested in, which is usually best-sellers. Many children's book authors are embarrassed when their friends say they can't find the book in their local bookstores, but this is a reality of the business. You should explain this to your friends and encourage them to ask the stores to order copies (but only if they sincerely intend to buy them).

It is about this time that Annabelle largely bows out of "selling" your book and turns it over to the marketing department, which handles publicity, promotion, and advertising. At Bench Press the marketing department consists of three people: the director and two assistants. What are their functions?

It's often said that publicity is free advertising, and promotion is paid advertising, including media ads, posters, bookmarks, and other giveaways. Little publicity is ever "free," but a publicist has been preparing the way for your book to go to about three hundred reviewers around the country. *Eating Dogfood Is No Fun* will land on the desks of reviewers for *The New York Times, Boston Globe, Washington Post, The Christian Science Monitor*, the *New Orleans Times Picayune, St. Louis Post-Dispatch, Dallas Herald*, the *Oregonian*, the *Los Angeles Times*, the *Asbury Park Press*, and scores of other papers that regularly review children's books, including *Kirkus Reviews*, a newsletter sent to libraries and some bookstores. *Eating Dogfood* will also go to the major magazines and other media, including some TV talk shows. But most important for children's books, it will be targeted at the school and library review journals, which are read by the potential buyers of most hardcover children's books.

Except for *Kirkus*, which is the only medium that reviews books before publication, other reviews will begin to appear around the publication date of *Eating Dogfood*; some reviews in specialized institutional media may take as long as eighteen months to surface. Annabelle will send them to you as they come in from the publicity department, which subscribes to a clipping service; you will be amazed at where your book ends up being reviewed. Of course, if your book is singled out for special attention, such as getting a starred (*) *Booklist* or pointered (♦) *Kirkus*, Annabelle will probably call you to share the good news.

Some of the reviews will be good ones, but you may also receive stupid or bad reviews. One review in *School Library Journal*, of a nonfiction book about the Southwest, did nothing but deplore the misspelling of a nineteenth-century Mexican general's name. When I called the author, she told me that her sources—both primary and secondary—gave three different spellings of the general's name, and she chose the one she thought was best. This was a stupid review, because the reviewer made heavy weather over a *fact* she *thought* was wrong. In such a case the editor or the author should write to the publication to clear up the matter.

However, if the offending review states a matter of *opinion* ("the characters never come to life," for example) do not write to the reviewer in protest. The first review I ever received was so malicious, tears came to my eyes. The second one, from a small newspaper in West Virginia, said my book was "gripping," and it almost wiped out the hurt from the first. Finally, a long, thoughtful review appeared in a professional journal, and I regained my equanimity. Bad reviews are part of the price we pay for being writers, and, though they never stop hurting, we have to take them in stride. By the way, at least two journals, *The Horn Book* and *Booklist*, make it a matter of policy to print only reviews of books that they recommend. If they don't wish to recommend a book, they simply don't review it.

Reviews are important not only for their effect on the writer (sometimes they are constructive and can help you improve your writing) but also because they bring your book to the attention of potential buyers. Children's publishers have small advertising budgets. Bench Press allows only $1,500 per book, which is used up quickly. Some money is spent on "list ads," which are ads appearing in the professional media listing all the books Bench Press published in a season. Once your book has some positive reviews, Bench Press will take out one or two small space ads for your book in the professional media. By this time, the advertising budget is exhausted.

You can use your own money to publicize your book in a way that doesn't conflict with what your publisher is doing. You can hire a professional publicist, but that is expensive, and not usually cost-effective for a children's book. However, you can make up your own press kit, which is a folder with a five-by-seven-inch black-and-white photo, and articles by you or about you or your book. Contact your local newspapers; they are always looking for "human interest" and may be delighted to go to your house and interview you. You can write your own author's bio and have a local printer design and print a black-and-white brochure or bookmark, which you can distribute when you make author's appearances or give to your local libraries and bookstores as a "point-of-purchase" giveaway. When you visit your local bookstores, speak to everyone there, not just the managers. You can also buy mailing lists and send out order forms for your book, but this is expensive; the list, postage, stationery, and printing might cost up to a dollar a name. If you decide to do this, be sure to check with your publisher about order fulfillment, unless you want to store boxes of books in your attic and spend your free time typing labels and packing books to mail out on your own. Some publishers provide publicity handbooks to their authors; find out whether yours does.

From before the time *Eating Dogfood* is published to well after publication, however, the marketing department is at work. Key bookstore accounts will receive bound galleys of your book, if the sales or marketing director thinks this will help. The marketing director cannot afford to lose her credibility with the bookstores or run over her budget, so only certain books will go this route. As a first novel, *Eating Dogfood* doesn't merit a poster or other special giveaway, but it will be on display at the various trade shows during the year, most especially the American Book Association convention, which is held every spring and is attended by bookstore buyers.

In addition, school and library promotion will make up for what the trade (bookstore) marketing lacks. Each year dozens of conferences and conventions are held on the international, national, and local levels, and are attended by librarians, reading teachers, English teachers, writers, and so forth.

The most important of these is the American Library Association (ALA), which holds a small working meeting in January (Midwinter) and a mammoth annual conference around June. Other important conferences are held by the International Reading Association (IRA), which also has state meetings; the National Council of Teachers of English (NCTE); and state meetings of local library and reading associations, such as the Texas Library Association (TLA) and the New England Library Association, NELA. At the beginning of each year the SCBW *Bulletin* publishes the "Calendar of Children's Book Exhibits and Events"—almost two hundred meetings!—compiled by Jim Roginski. Publishers attend the most important of these meetings.

Annabelle and other editors might go to the midwinter ALA or the summer ALA; at the least, the editorial director of children's books will attend both. ABA is primarily a sales and marketing convention, so few editors attend, unless the meeting is in New York City or Washington, D.C. The editorial director seems to spend all his time traveling in the spring and fall, when these meetings take place, in addition to holding the three sales conferences.

Attending conferences is one activity that keeps Annabelle out of the office so much, because she'll often fill in for her boss when he has a conflict, especially in April, when TLA, sales conference, and the Bologna Book Fair have been known to coincide. Bologna is an event the subsidiary rights director can't miss: it's an important opportunity to sell rights to foreign publishers. At the smallest, local conferences, only sales reps may attend. If at all possible, you, the writer, should try to attend some of these conventions to see what is happening. Later in your career, Bench Press may invite you to be its guest, but in the beginning, don't count on it.

What happens at these conventions? Whether it's ABA, ALA, or a tiny state library association conference, Bench Press sets up its booth, a place where recent books are displayed, and where representatives from the firm can stand and chat with potential buyers. Attendance at ALA runs around 15,000 or more, including exhibitors and librarians. Held at the biggest convention centers in cities like Chicago, Los Angeles, New Orleans, San Francisco, Philadelphia, Atlanta, or Dallas, the ALA features aisles full of hundreds of booths of books and library equipment, from computers to furniture. Even the Library of Congress has a booth!

A great deal of entertaining takes place, as publishers invite librarians to meet authors and illustrators at breakfasts, lunches, cocktail parties, dinners, and nightcaps. Especially sought after as guests are the members of the various award-giving committees of the ALA, such as the Newbery, Caldecott, Notable Book, and the Young Adult Services Division committees. This gives publishers and librarians (many of whom head state or municipal library systems) a chance to talk about books and authors in relaxed surroundings.

At the booths, authors and illustrators will autograph their new books. Choosing which author or illustrator will attend depends, usually, on their having a new book to display and sign, or a recent book that has won an award. The lines are long at the booths of those publishers whose authors and artists have won either a Newbery or Caldecott Medal for that year or who have an especially popular author on hand.

Although it is smaller, the Midwinter ALA is as important as the summer one. All during the year, committee members have been reading and discussing the new books. At the conventions they get together to go over the lists and make preliminary nominations for the prizes. But it's at Midwinter that final decisions are reached and editors are told the results. Editors with prizewinning books race for the telephones to call their authors or illustrators with the news, sometimes even at four in the morning.

Winning the Caldecott Medal or Honor Book status will increase sales of a book dramatically. The same is true of the Newbery, though to a lesser extent. Notable Books or YASD Best Books used to sell noticeably better after winning the prizes, but this has been less so lately. Still, awards make the publisher and the author happy, and influence sales somewhat. Getting a Notable or Best Book designation also brings the book to the attention of more people, and may be the first step to a bigger award for another book by that author later. The Newbery and Caldecott medals are formally presented at a gala dinner during the summer ALA.

That's not all. The publicity department at Bench Press has also sent *Eating Dogfood* to other award committees all over the country, most especially to the many state library or reading associations that award state prizes. Groups in Iowa, Utah, Arizona, and other states draw up master lists of books for the children in their states to read and vote on. Although it's wonderful to win the Texas Bluebonnet Award or the Hawaii Nene Award or the New Hampshire Dorothy Canfield Fisher Award, it's just as wonderful to be on the master list, since many copies of the book are purchased for the children to read. This is a splendid boost to sales as well as to your ego.

Awards come from many directions, and some of the best known are the *Boston Globe–Horn Book* Award, the SCBW Golden Kite Award, the Christopher Award, the *New York Times* Ten Best-Illustrated Children's Book Award, and the *School Library Journal* "Best Books" list. The National Council of Social Studies Teachers and the National Council of Science Teachers also draw up lists of the best books in those disciplines. The New York Public Library recommends books in its annual Books for the Teen-Age selection. And all you had to do was write a good book! The publicity department at Bench Press did the rest.

The joy of publishing continues. Reference book publishers may invite you to contribute a brief autobiography to such volumes as *Something about the Author, Contemporary Authors,* or *Who's Who.* The first two will publish your biography at no charge, but I learned from experience that *Who's Who* (which publishes a number of different directories) will use the material only if you promise to buy the volume with your material in it.

Other invitations may arrive, to speak at schools or before library groups or writers. It's important that you refer all such invitations to the publicity department. First, you should discuss your speaking fees with the publicist. When you are first published, it seems exciting to speak at a local school. But after you've done it a few times, you will realize you are spending valuable time away from your writing. Not only are you not getting paid for your work, you are paying your own travel and meal expenses. It's not a bad idea to do it a few times for free, especially near your hometown, to get the practice and to polish your act. But after that you should at least arrange to have travel and meals paid for. As time goes on and your fame grows, you can begin to ask for fees ranging from as little as fifty dollars to a thousand. Many juvenile authors have enhanced their careers and their incomes by going on the road. Since so little money is available for advertising, this sort of self-promotion is extremely valuable.

If you are shy and have a romantic vision of being an artist starving in a garret, you must realize that writing books that sell is a business. You can help your book to sell better by going out in the world and projecting warmth, energy, and confidence to your readers. When you meet your public for the first time, leave your jewels and furs or T-shirt and jeans at home and dress in a businesslike way, taking care with your wardrobe and makeup.

It's important that your publisher be involved in your travel plans, which is a given if the invitation comes through the publisher; indeed, the publicist will even suggest your name to some inquirers. Although it's flattering to be invited directly, always tell the prospective host that she must get in touch with your publisher before you can accept the invitation. First, having to deal with the publisher puts the host on notice that you are a professional, not just a sweet person who's willing to talk to their group. Second, the publicist can advise you on an appropriate fee. Third, she can warn you about places where other authors have had unpleasant experiences. Fourth, it is she who will order copies of your book (for sale and autographing) to be sent to the place you are speaking.

Authors swap horror stories with one another and with publicists, so word soon got around when a host made an author speak to thirty classes of children (none of whom had ever heard of him or read his book) in six schools in two days. To add to the horror, the author had to sleep on a bumpy sofa bed in the host's house—and the host had three children under five who cried all the time. And only one bathroom.

Be sure to double-check everything and assume nothing. Once I was invited to speak at a sprawling major university located off a highway in the middle of nowhere. After a delicious dinner in town, my hosts dropped me off at the campus hotel. However, the next morning I discovered that no arrangements had been made to pick me up, and neither the hotel nor I had any idea where the talk was being held, nor did I have a way to get there, even if I knew. Yet other hosts went out of their way to ensure my comfort, down to champagne and roses in a luxury hotel. It's always an adventure to go on the road.

Helen Cavanagh, speaking at a writer's conference, gave the following advice. "You are your product," she said. "Prepare yourself by writing down every question an interviewer might ask. If you go on TV (local stations welcome local authors), wear bright red or blue close to your face. Cross your legs, but not at the knees. Don't wiggle. Don't make faces. And set ground rules: say you won't answer certain kinds of personal questions." She also suggested getting a professional publicity photograph, showing you to be the kind of person your reader imagines you to be.

Another joy for the writer is to receive mail, especially from children. Some receive so much mail that they need a secretary to handle it. Others ask publicity departments to send back a form letter, especially to children who are writing and asking for information for a book report. Be warned: the most common questions children ask are: How much money do you make? and How long did it take you to write the book? Have your answers ready.

Far less pleasant is "hate mail." I'm not referring to the occasional parent who writes out of concern for his child and objects to something you've said. You can answer these people with candor and sincerity. By hate mail I mean mail from people with axes to grind, preferably on books deemed to be offensive by various groups. I'm talking about censorship.

At Nat Hentoff shows in his novel *The Day They Came To Arrest the Book*, censors can descend from any direction, right or left. On the right are the religious zealots who object to the mention of Christmas trees (because they're pagan) and evolution (because it's not in the Bible). On the left are some feminists, members of various ethnic groups, "health nuts," and those concerned about animal rights, from paramecia up, and other causes.

Some sales reps, teachers, librarians, and parents want children's publishers to put a designation on each book similar to what the movie industry does for movies. At sales conferences, I've heard reps ask whether the words "damn" or "hell" appeared in my books. "You've got to tell us," they say, "because I can't sell those books in my territory. If I don't know, and the librarians find the words, we lose our credibility." Teachers, parents, and librarians have returned books they found offensive. "You didn't tell us the book had street language," they say. On the other hand, as editors and writers, is it our responsibility to warn people about "offensive" material in books?

First, let's look into what has been deemed offensive in children's books during the last twenty years.

One morning at Viking Press, I was surprised to receive a letter from a teacher in California stating that *Whistle in the Graveyard* by the noted folkorist Maria Leach (which I had edited and was proud of) had been removed from his school library. The teacher had read aloud the North Carolina folktale "How To Become a Witch," about a man named Nick who discovered that the way to become a witch was to stand in a "magic circle" and chant this rhyme:

> *Devil take me*
> *Devil take the ring*
> *Devil take me*
> *And everything.*

When the ground began to sink beneath his feet, Nick jumped up and out of the circle and ran home as fast as he could: he'd decided he didn't want to be a witch after all.

According to the teacher, one of his students began to cry hysterically when the teacher read the chant, because the boy believed the devil was on his way to the classroom. The parents of the boy demanded the book be removed from the school. The teacher asked for our help, because the school was going to hold a hearing. To support him in his contention that the book was suitable for class use, we sent him copies of the many good reviews from professional media and a brief biography of Maria Leach, who was also the author of scholarly works about folklore. We also suggested he get in touch with the American Library Association Committee on Intellectual Freedom, and heard no more of the case. But we were stunned that a traditional tale, meant partly as joke and partly as a caution *against* meddling with evil, had caused so much trouble. It was not the folktale that was at fault, but the parents of the child who had so frightened him that a passage in a book could bring on hysterics.

Not long afterward, I attended a meeting of the Author's Guild and heard about the danger of using the word "evolution" in a book for children. "It's all right to talk about the theory," the speaker said, "just don't use the word, because the book will be banned." That sounded truly ridiculous. I'd seen *Inherit the Wind* and believed that the shenanigans of the infamous Scopes trial had laid that bugaboo to rest fifty years before. (The pro-evolution teacher had lost the case, but by the seventies, wasn't the play just of historical interest? It couldn't happen again, could it?)

Another speaker at the Author's Guild said she had written a book with a strong anti-hunting theme. Since then, she said, she'd been "deluged with hate mail from members of the National Rifle Association." It is called "hate mail" because the language in it is often vicious and ugly.

The sixties had been a time when writers for children had broken the old taboos, and a new freedom and honesty about sex had appeared in children's books. Dick and Jane were dead, editors and writers thought, and we could publish books about children and society that were accurate reflections of today's world. But sex was not the issue in the instances mentioned earlier, although it was important in other cases. This new censorship grew like a cancer, and nothing was safe to write about. Books began to disappear from library shelves, quietly. Or offending pages were cut out, quietly. However, when the work of censoring was done in broad daylight, the censors often lost out.

"Most people who attempt to have books banned dislike being called censors," wrote Edward B. Jenkinson in his 1979 book *Censors in the Classroom*. This was certainly true of Mel Gabler. "Those who bring textbook content to the public's attention are often referred to as 'textbook censors,' " he wrote. "However, this is not true. Traditional American values are now being censored from textbooks even before they reach the reviewer." Mel Gabler and his wife, Norma, had been reviewing textbooks since 1961, and informing their followers—in Texas and elsewhere—about books that should not be adopted for school use because they contained material that did not promote those "traditional American values." Publishers, who depend on state-wide adoptions, began to rewrite textbooks to remove such material as Edgar Allan Poe's "gruesome poem, 'The Raven,' " statements that imply man is an animal, and dictionaries with "vulgar language and unreasonable definitions." Most chilling was the advice the Gablers gave to sympathetic parents, which was, according to Jenkinson, that they did not have to read entire books to review them, only the "questioned" parts selected by the Gablers.

But the Gablers' activities began to be noticed by others, including Frances Fitzgerald, who wrote a long, detailed article about them in the *New Yorker*. The struggle for free speech in books for children (and adults) was on.

In the seventies and eighties, hundreds of local, state, and national groups descended on schools and libraries nationwide, demanding that books be banned. They were sometimes successful, sometimes not. For example, the Texas Library Association began a long and successful court battle on the issue of whether books on creationism should be shelved in the science section. One librarian showed me a textbook where, she said, "They took evolution out of the text, but forgot to take it out of the index."

In spite of the successes, we knew that children's books were vulnerable targets. Editors began to warn authors about material that would draw the attention of censors, and reviewers began to flag objectionable material, which affected sales. Bookstores refused to carry certain books, and award committees allowed members' prejudices to influence their selections. Most alarming, writers began to censor themselves.

No one questions a parent's right to oversee his child's moral welfare. And our society accepts a plurality of religious beliefs. In all instances of censorship, the question has been whether *others* have a right to prevent you or your child from reading what they consider harmful. Although the Catholic Legion of Decency told me, when I was a girl, that it was a sin to read *The Life of Martin Luther* or the King James Bible, it did not remove those books from public libraries.

It was in one of the world's great children's books, *Tom Sawyer*, that Mark Twain wrote about human contrariness, and the example holds true in relation to censorship. As Tom is whitewashing the fence, which he hates doing, he tells his friends they can't have the same fun he is having. You know what happens next: his friends whitewash the fence for him. Censors fall into the "contrariness" trap, over and over again.

It's ironic that Twain's *The Adventures of Huckleberry Finn* is one of our most censored of books because it contains a "demeaning" picture of women, a black man called Nigger Jim, and Huck and Jim cavorting naked on the raft. A nonracist version by John H. Wallace became available in 1983, but as Roger Sutton, writing in *School Library Journal*, points out about this "sivilizing" of Huck, "Twain's stern moral vision, his irony—the reasons this book are taught—are gone."

The Council of Interracial Books for Children did monumental work in the seventies, pointing out that history books, especially, neglected the roles of women, blacks, and other "minorities," while perpetuating the view that everything worthwhile had been done by white heterosexual males of north European descent. But as with so many worthy movements, the CIBC began to get silly, too, in its objections to books. They deplored Rosa Guy's *Edith Jackson* because the protagonist didn't use birth control (which was the point of the book!).

The question of the Doctor Dolittle books is a particularly thorny one, highlighting the conflict writers and editors feel about objectionable material for children.

The CIBC condemned Doctor Dolittle on racist grounds. However, *all* the Dolittle books were banned from many libraries although only two had material that could be labeled racist. *The Story of Doctor Dolittle* had a chapter about Prince Bumpo, an African who painted himself white; some drawings depicted Africans with exaggerated Negroid features, and one showed Prince Bumpo sleeping on a bench (implying that Africans were lazy). Some of the books also used the words "Red man," for Native American, which was common usage in England at the time the books were written. "The CIBC ignored the fact that Bumpo went on to graduate from Oxford," Christopher Lofting, Hugh Lofting's son and literary executor, told me. "The only other person who was the doctor's intellectual equal was a 'savage' [another censored word] from the Pacific Islands." Lofting was particularly irate at the fact that the CIBC had called for libraries and other book buyers to boycott all of J. B. Lippincott's books, including their many medical and legal texts, saying Lippincott was a "racist publisher."

Lofting reluctantly agreed to edit the books, removing the offending words, chapter, and art and adding drawings by his father that had never been published. "These new versions come after a lot of soul-searching," said Lofting in an interview when the books were republished by Delacorte/Dell in the 1980s. "Publishers should not be in the business of censorship. You don't lightly tamper with a classic. My father would have been astonished and outraged at some of the accusations leveled at him."

In an editorial, the London *Times* deplored the new editions: "Self-assumed moral and intellectual superiority, born of a current political fashion, visits an intolerable impertinence on the original authors, and an even greater one on the potential readers. It credits today's young people with neither intelligence nor perception."

On the other hand, without editing, the books would have been kept out of the hands of generations of American children. None of the books was still in print in the United States, though they were available in the original formats from Jonathan Cape and Penguin in England.

If you were an editor, would you reissue for children Booth Tarkington's *Penrod*, which was considered a classic when I was a child? An African American friend told me it is "permeated with the aroma of racism." (It hadn't seemed that way to me when I was young.) In one scene Penrod feeds a home brew containing arsenic and paint thinner to a boy he dislikes, who may be Jewish. (I knew better than to drink poison, and the character's possible religion was of no interest to me.) The book also has a fair amount of cruelty to animals (which was to be expected, I thought, from boys). What I do remember feeling—as a child—was that the book was a condescending look at boyhood from an adult point of view and laughed at children instead of with them. Do we trust today's children enough to let them make up their own minds about this book? Suppose a new manuscript turned up with the same sort of material in it? Would you publish it as is or ask for changes?

The question remains: where do writers and editors draw the line about offensive material? The following topics have also come under attack in recent years: ice cream (because some say it is a junk food); unsympathetic characters (a nasty teacher who is Jewish) belonging to an identifiable ethnic, religious, or racial group; a *sym-*

pathetic character (a Chinese servant in 1900 who speaks pidgin English) belonging to an identifiable ethnic, religious, or racial group; the use of "darn" or "heck" or "my goodness" (because they stand for stronger words); witches, second sight, astrology, or other "occult" matters; any child (Pollyanna) defying adult authority; an unflattering portrait of a stepmother or stepfather; toilet training and language; "secular humanism"; homosexual relationships (happy or unhappy); hunting (fishing?); humorous comments about members of certain professions (as in "all nurses are sex maniacs"). . . .

Well-meaning people have always believed that children's books have a duty to bend young minds in the "right" directions. But others agree with Russell Baker, who wrote in one of his columns, "Education involves training people to think clearly. [It is not] a propaganda system to be manipulated for transient social or political purposes. Which is to say, with contempt."

Nonetheless, children's writers and editors sit *in loco parentis.* We do have a responsibility toward young, suggestible minds. As we would not feed a child arsenic, we cannot feed it mental poison either. Long before a book is published, several people have read it, including the editor, whose function is to decide whether a book is well written. But his personal values will affect his decision, too. Several editors declined Robert Cormier's *The Chocolate War,* because of personal taste (it had a pessimistic ending). Once a book is published, reviewers will examine it for sexism, racism, and other -isms; declared guilty, a book will suffer. Many teachers and librarians are reluctant to purchase books that may cause trouble with various groups. And many bookstores won't carry books dealing with sex because they, too, fear upsetting parents.

It is easy to forget that literature *should* be subversive, showing the underside of the human condition, the truth about people and life. Artists have a valuable, unique vision of reality that is often at odds with community standards. Yesterday's banned book is often today's classic, and yesterday's classic is banned today.

Censorship has been around for centuries: remember what happened to Socrates. Each society has its standards. Each person has his own. When they clash, censorship is likely. It will remain with us, and the Supreme Court will continue to pass judgment on particular cases involving the First Amendment. Therefore if you choose to write something others will consider "offensive," be prepared to lose sales and to defend your book when it is publicly removed from the shelves.

Should one of your books be attacked, get in touch with your editor immediately. She will lend you moral support and suggest ways you can get help from various organizations, including the Committee on Intellectual Freedom of the American Library Association and the National Coalition against Censorship. As the author, you must get involved in protecting your First Amendment rights. If the case against your book is made public, you're ahead of the game, because most people are against self-appointed censors. And you won't be alone, because so many other writers for children have gone before you into the fray. Every year the ALA holds its "Banned Book Week," when books that have been censored go on display in libraries all over the country. The sight of these well-known books is an eye-opener, and you'll be surprised at what you'll see there. Talk about being in exalted company!

Publishing means "to make public," and going public can be a great deal of fun. Writing is a lonely craft, and being out among your fans and peers—and critics—is exhilarating; you can hear the applause not just in your own mind or in the reviews but from a living, laughing audience. After speaking in public, you'll have a new energy for your real work, the writing.

But your true audience is always the children. I couldn't wait to learn to read, and I still remember daring to make my first trip to the public library on my own. I knew which bus to take to get there, but when I came out of the library, loaded down with books, I had no idea where to catch the bus for the return trip. So I walked home, about a mile, dying to dive into those books.

Can any other career surpass writing and publishing books for children, who so value books they'd walk a mile to get them? Contrary to popular belief, teaching may well be the oldest profession, with storytelling next, because both are of supreme importance to the human continuum. Through books we will pass on the best we have to the next generation. If we're lucky, we'll be remembered for a long, long time.

IMPORTANT ADDRESSES

ORGANIZATIONS

American Book Producers Association
41 Union Square West, Room 1327
New York, NY 10003

The Children's Book Council
568 Broadway, Suite 404
New York, NY 10012

Committee on Intellectual Freedom
American Library Association
50 East Huron Street
Chicago, IL 60611

International Reading Association
800 Barksdale Road
PO Box 8139
Newark, DE 19714-8139

National Coalition Against Censorship
2 West 64th Street
New York, NY 10023

Society of Children's Book Writers
PO Box 66296
Mar Vista Station
Los Angeles, CA 90066

PUBLICATIONS

Booklist
50 East Huron Street
Chicago, IL 60611

The Horn Book
14 Beacon Street
Boston, MA 02108

Publisher's Weekly
PO Box 1979
Marion, OH 43306-2079

School Library Journal
Reader Service Department
PO Box 5670
Denver, CO 80217-9527

VOYA
1226 Cresthaven Drive
Silver Spring, MD 20903

The Writer
120 Boylston Street
Boston, MA 02116

Writer's Digest
PO Box 2124
Harlan, IA 51593-2313

SUGGESTED READING

The list below is by no means a complete one, but it will serve as an introduction to children's literature, publishing, and writing for children. Many of the titles below have their own bibliographies, and you will soon be compiling your own list of treasured books.

Aldiss, Brian W., with David Wingrove. *Trillion Year Spree: The History of Science Fiction*. New York: Atheneum, 1986; Avon Books, 1988.

An analysis of the trends, theories, and current practices of this rich and varied genre, including references to Lewis Carroll, Ursula K. LeGuin, Anne McCaffrey, Joan Vinge, and others who have written fantasy and science fiction for young people.

Arbuthnot, May Hill, and Dorothy M. Broderick, Shelton L. Root, Jr., Mark Taylor, and Evelyn L. Wenzel. *The Arbuthnot Anthology of Children's Literature*. Glenview, Ill.: Scott, Foresman, 1973.

A book for browsing and reference, containing selections (with commentaries) of poetry, folklore, fiction, and nonfiction. An excellent introduction to the best of children's literature.

Blinn, Marjeanne Jensen, compiler. *Summoned by Books: Essays and Speeches by Frances Clarke Sayers*. New York: Viking, 1965.

Sayers, a librarian, storyteller, and teacher, celebrates children's books with passion and wisdom.

Bonn, Thomas L. *Undercover: An Illustrated History of American Mass Market Paperbacks*. Foreword by John Tebbel. New York: Penguin, 1982.

A lively history of the evolution of paperbacks, with particular emphasis on cover art.

Burack, Sylvia K., ed. *The Writer's Handbook*. Boston: The Writer, 1986.

Essays on writing by 162 writers for adults and children with lists of publishers, literary agents, writers' organizations, contests, awards, and grants for writers.

The Chicago Manual of Style: For Authors, Editors, and Copywriters. Chicago: University of Chicago Press, 1982.

The fundamentals of preparing manuscripts for printers, especially valuable for writers of nonfiction.

Field, Syd. *The Screenwriter's Workbook*. New York: Dell, 1984.

Useful for its compact advice on structure, characterization, and dialog.

Flower, Mary. *A Writer's Guide to a Children's Book Contract*. Brooklyn, N.Y.: Fern Hill Books, 1988.

Explains "clause by clause, the language and steps necessary for every author to understand what is being signed *before signing*"—Jim Roginski.

Follett, Wilson, and Jacques Barzun, eds. *Modern American Usage: A Guide*. New York: Hill and Wang, 1966.

The American companion to Fowler's *Modern English Usage*.

Fowler, H. W. *A Dictionary of Modern English Usage*. New York: Oxford University Press, 1963.

"The most valuable advice you can give young writers today is: 'Learn your language.' . . . You must own a copy"—Evelyn Waugh.

Giblin, James Cross. *Writing Books for Young People*. Boston: The Writer, 1990.

An editor and writer discusses writing for children, with an especially useful section on nonfiction.

Greenfeld, Howard. *Books: From Writer to Reader*. New York: Crown, 1976.

A clear description of how a book is produced. Written for young people, it can be profitably read by adults as well.

Healy, Jane M. *Endangered Minds: Why Our Children Don't Think*. New York: Simon & Schuster, 1990.

A disturbing book by an educational psychologist arguing that changes in brain structure, caused by contemporary life, are responsible for children's decreased ability to think and read.

Jenkinson, Edward B. *Censors in the Classroom: The Mind Benders*. Carbondale and Edwardsville, Ill.: Southern Illinois University Press, 1979.

A chilling account of book censorship, including the works of children's writers such as Judy Blume, Nat Hentoff, and Paul Zindel. The book also contains concrete suggestions for countering the censors.

Lurie, Alison. *Don't Tell the Grown-ups: Subversive Children's Literature.* Boston: Little, Brown, 1990.

A rewarding collection of essays.

Opie, Robert and Iona, and Brian Alderson. *The Treasures of Childhood: Books, Toys, and Games from the Opie Collection.* New York: Arcade, 1989.

Lavishly illustrated in full color, this is an entertaining and authoritative look at antique novelty books for children.

Polking, Kirk, Joan Bloss, and Colleen Cannon, eds. *Writer's Encyclopedia.* Cincinnati: Writer's Digest Books, 1983.

Answers to your writing and publishing questions arranged alphabetically.

Postman, Neil. *The Disappearance of Childhood.* New York: Dell, 1982.

A history of childhood, from antiquity to the present, with grave warnings about society's current attitudes toward children.

Prager, Arthur. *Rascals at Large, or, the Clue in the Old Nostalgia.* Garden City: Doubleday, 1971.

An entertaining and affectionate look at why series books of the past were so appealing to young readers.

Seuling, Barbara. *How To Write a Children's Book and Get It Published.* New York: Scribner's, 1991.

An inspiring guide to writing for children with chapters on poetry, plays, and illustration.

Shulevitz, Uri. *Writing with Pictures: How To Write and Illustrate Children's Books.* New York: Watson-Guptill, 1985.

Designed to help the artist understand the technical and esthetic aspects of illustrating children's books.

Skillen, Marjorie, E. *Words into Type.* Englewood Cliffs, N.J.: Prentice-Hall, 1974.

Answers the questions writers of fiction may have about the fine points of punctuating dialog and other arcane matters. An indispensable desk reference for all copy editors and writers.

Strunk, William, Jr. *The Elements of Style*. New York: Macmillan, 1959.

A terse and invaluable guide for writers.

Swain, Dwight V. *Techniques of the Selling Writer*. Norman: University of Oklahoma Press, 1974.

Reissued by popular demand, a thorough guide to the craft of writing.

Townsend, John Rowe. *Written for Children: An Outline of English-language Children's Literature*. New York: Lippincott, 1983.

An enjoyable and sometimes controversial account of the development of children's books in Britain and the United States.

Webster's Dictionary of English Usage. Springfield, Mass.: Merriam-Webster, 1989.

Webster's New Dictionary of Synonyms: A Dictionary of Discriminated Synonyms with Antonyms and Analogous and Contrasted Words. Springfield, Mass.: Merriam-Webster, 1984.

Webster's Ninth New Collegiate Dictionary. Springfield, Mass.: Merriam-Webster, 1986.

Whitney, Phyllis A. *Writing Juvenile Stories and Novels: How To Write and Sell Fiction for Young People*. Boston: The Writer, 1976.

Step-by-step instruction in writing fiction for young people, with a chapter on writing juvenile mysteries.

Yolen, Jane. *Guide to Writing for Children*. Boston: The Writer, 1989.

Authoritative and engaging, with an emphasis on the importance of storytelling.

INDEX